WHEN HELL BECOMES YOUR HOME:

HOW I SURVIVED 14 YEARS IN PRISON

Author N. Cognito

An elite U.S. soldier, sent to a notorious prison, must survive by relying upon his advanced military training and learning to be a convict the hard way: trial and error.

Drawing upon his hard earned experiences, gained in an unforgiving world, the author shares his knowledge for the benefit of others without them having to walk through the same purgatorial paths themselves.

Jason Schultz: Close Combat Instructor with the Gung Ho Chuan Association.

"Let his 14 years of Hell become your salvation. The author, Mr. N. Cognito set out to simply write what he terms a prison survival guide but what he has given us so much more. "When Hell Becomes Your Home" is an easy but rather deep read. I don't mean easy as in elementary, easy as in when you read it you can feel the author taking you under his wing, guiding you step by step on how to survive the Demon Farm. After the first time you read it, put it down. Let everything digest. After a few weeks or months pick it up again and revisit the chapters that interest you. You'll find deeper meaning to the Author's words. Here is where you will find the real power in his words. This book was intended to be a prison survival guide but it may as well be a life survival guide. Every lesson he learned and has shared within these pages can be overlaid on each of our lives. Our lives in the free world are just as easily impacted by the predators and psychic vampires you'd expect to find behind bars. I am thankful to have come across this author so that I might learn from him, you should do the same."

Clint Jahn:

"His (Author N. Cognito's) opinions and observations are just as interesting as his core concepts."

Alex Kruz: Actor, director, stuntman, U.S. Army veteran.

" Very good read and there is an increasing need for this kind of information in the world today...Hoo-ah"

Rhe Vatone: Federal Correction Officer.

"I have read this book three times and now I am going back through it with a highlighter marker. Some of these things we learned in our training but a lot of the things in this book are new and very informative. I have learned a lot from this book."

ISBN 978-1-312-70119-9

WHEN HELL BECOMES YOUR HOME:
HOW I SURVIVED 14YEARS IN PRISON

BY: AUTHOR N. COGNITO.

ISBN 978-1-312-70119-9

WARNING

The author, the editor, and the publisher are not and will not be responsible, in anyway whatsoever, for any use made by anyone, whether proper or improper, of the information contained in this book. All use of the aforementioned information must be made in accordance with what is permitted by law, and damage liable to be caused as a result thereof, will be the exclusive responsibility of the user.

CONTENTS

INTRODUCTION.

Ch. 1. Psychology of Survival and Battle-Proofing the Mind.

Ch. 2. Awareness, Adaptation, and Fabricating a Positive Attitude.

Ch. 3. Enduring Hardship and Suffering.

Ch. 4. Concrete Jungle and Unwritten Rules.

Ch. 5. Self-Defense and Physical Training.

Ch. 6. Looking For A Few Real Men.

Ch. 7. Hustlers, Cons, and Psychic Vampires.

CONCLUSION.

INTRODUCTION

This book is for the 'fresh fish' (newly incarcerated) facing a short time or an extended stay in the penitentiary. But it will serve just as well for the incarcerated in jails and detention camps.

I did not have the benefit of such an informative manual when I was taken out of the U.S. Army, away from my woman and child, and sent to prison. So I had to draw upon my military training, my wits, and my faith in Creator (God). I had to adapt and overcome.

Experience is a cruel and hard teacher, so I've written this book with the goal of saving some individual from having to walk blindly into the pitfalls that await the inexperienced in prison by sharing a combination of military training and convict wisdom gained from over a decade of experience, surviving the demon farm that they call PRISON.

It is my hope that this book will save lives and provide someone's son or daughter with the tools and wisdom to survive prison. Hopefully they will grow and better themselves through opposition and adversity. Just as coal may become a stronger, more valuable, creation through intense heat and pressure over long periods of time, so does the human soul have the potential to become something greater through even the most unbearable trials if one so chooses. The same things that will break you will make you.

As a final note: If you happen to be incarcerated for preying upon children, **while knowing in your heart you're guilty of such actions,** please do not disgrace this book by reading it's pages. Your redemption, as with all, lies only with the Creator.

To all the truly innocent and wrongfully incarcerated, to all the one's incarcerated for self-defense or defense of love ones, and to all of my Infantry brothers in arms, my heart and prayers go out to you all. Peace and freedom be upon you.

And to my family, friends, relations, indigenous american brothers and sisters, relatives in the faith, and my dear son Emmanuel-Manuelito-, I love you altruistically.

Creator Tsisas bless you all eternally. One day we will meet again.

HOO-AH

Prisoner #320019, 9 Oct 2012

Chapter 1.

PSYCHOLOGY OF SURVIVAL

AND

BATTLEPROOFING THE MIND

Any survival instructor will tell you that the main mental keys to survival in any situation are Awareness, Adaptability, and Positive Attitude. These three keys unlock the doors to every other aspect to survival.

Psychologically you want to **adapt** to the situation as quickly as possible and **overcome** the situation. In prison they say, "Do the time~don't let the time do you." But before we can perform this way we must decide in our heart do we want to survive. Do we want to be a victim of our circumstance or an active survivor. By now you're probably incarcerated, lost your freedom, your job/career, your respectability, maybe your home, worldly possessions, and all of your money. And maybe you've even lost the things that matter to you more than your own life; your family, your wife, and your children. Maybe the foul spirit of hopelessness and despair has gripped your heart and mind so that you just want to sleep and never wake up again.

Perhaps you're being attacked with thoughts of suicide and ways to do it with what is at hand. Perhaps you have lost all desire to eat, drink, bathe, or or even get up and face another day. **This is depression.**

There is a saying of the big belly Buddha and there is psychological peace in it. "Give up this life in your mind and you will find peace. Learn to let go and you will find happiness." If you're trying to hold onto your free-world life and everything you feel slipping away, or that you were taken away from, then realize this is the root of your depression and detrimental to your survival. Letting go is easy. It's the holding on that's hard and creates suffering. Take comfort in this idea because in fact the harder you try to hold onto everyone and everything the faster you will see it slip away. You will in fact even push it away. Like water, the harder you grasp the more elusive it becomes. So learn to let go and you will find peace.

Many people in the free-world whom seem to have it all are actually living in a prison of the heart, mind, and emotions. And some people living in a physical prison of concrete and steel have found freedom within and inner peace...But it is a journey of a thousand miles that begins with one step.

Once you've decided that you want to survive for yourself, your loved ones, or for no other reason but to disappoint those who would rejoice at your destruction, then it is time to cultivate **the undying will to prevail.**

You only have two choices: Either get busy living or get busy dying. If you feel you have no reason to live and hate life, then think of your survival as an act of rebellion against your enemies. Leonardo Di Vinci said it best when he declared to the world, "Opposition only leads me to strong resolution."

In the military, soldiers of elite units are trained in counter-detention and resistance. It's very important psychologically to maintain one's personal hygiene, health, and fitness in order to combat the enemy of depression and illness (which enhances the pain of depression). You must exercise self-discipline and try to create some kind of routine. Studies show that maintaining a personal hygiene routine, keeping a clean living space, eating to keep up your strength, drinking water, and some routine of physical exercise, go far in reducing stress and combating depression. Also, it's a way to take back some personal control over your life in a world where you have lost most control of your life to others.

Maintaining personal hygiene gives one a positive clean feeling that has deep psychological effects and health benefits. A clean healthy body is a less stressful body. Eating to keep up one's strength keeps the body strong and therefore the mind strong. Our bodies are chemically dependent upon vitamins and enzymes we get from food, water, and even sunlight. Without it we become more susceptible to depression, psychosis, and illness. Keeping our personal space clean and our bodies physically fit with some form of exercise also acts as a form of physical and mental therapy. Besides the health benefits, chemically and psychologically it reduces all forms of stress and gives one a feeling of well being and euphoria. Exercise specifically releases **endorphins** which give one psychologically and physically a natural high. "A strong body-is a strong mind-is a strong heart." Drinking water also reduces stress, lowers blood pressure, and keeps the body and brain chemically balanced. Water, like air and sunlight, is crucial in maintaining physical and mental harmony. This contributes totally to your emotional well being and state of mind.

Breathing is not just an involuntary act but can be a very effective form of mental, emotional, and physical stress and pain reduction. The martial arts call it an internal exercise and Tibetan Buddhism's Shamatha discipline refers to it as the "taming of the mind." Modern medicine encourages breathing exercise for pain management and stress reduction, as does the U.S. military.

A simple exercise used by elite military units is called, COMBAT BREATHING. You will practice inhaling for four seconds and exhaling for six. It is important you inhale through the nose and exhale out of the mouth.

Oxygen is more readily absorbed through the surface capillaries in the sinus cavity before reaching the lungs, so more oxygen enters the bloodstream. And the carbon dioxide is more efficiently removed from the body exhaling out of the mouth. This Combat Breathing technique is used to restore normal heart rate, lower BP, reduce stress, calm nerves, and manage pain…It is very effective.

A very effective technique of coping with, or preparing for, the traumatic and stressful situation of combat (or prison) is called **Battle-Proofing the Mind.** This is a technique taught to elite military units and is similar to self-hypnosis, or reinforced positive visualization techniques, used by professional athletes. You may sit down for this exercise but it's more effective if you can lay down on your back comfortably and relax your body. You will close the eyes and begin your combat breathing exercise and allow your body to melt away. Your hands may be at your sides or folded gently over your belly. You will focus initially upon the inhale and exhale of the breath until you are completely relaxed. You should imagine you are separating from your environment, and if you feel detached from your body this is fine. You may now visualize yourself as being in the eye of the hurricane; the calm at the storm's center. Chaos and confusion is all around you but you reside always in the calm at the center. You will visualize that you can walk between the raindrops and not get wet. You may even visualize a placid blue body of water and the tide rolls in and out with your breath. The sky is baby blue and all your worries and fears are like clouds floating by. You watch them float by but you do not grasp them and hold onto them. You simply watch them go by as a passive observer and focus on the breath. You have become the breath and your thoughts are passers by.

Now you may take your mind and visualize all around you is warfare, chaos, violence, and horror. But within you is the eye of the hurricane; the calm at the center of the storm. When you go about your day and are surrounded by the storm and chaos of prison return to the breath. Like an ocean tide that ebbs and flows in and out; four and six. And visualize yourself in that place, you have no fear, no anger, no emotion, no foolish pride. You are the calm within the storm. You are humble, yet fearless and without form. They can not grab or subdue that which is formless. You are water; the harder it is grasped the more elusive it becomes. You are calm and elusive. Always return to the breath. Follow the breath. Become the breath.

You may tell yourself within that you are a survivor, a humble and wise warrior and maintaining the undying will to prevail in all things. Tell yourself you are a peaceful lion among wolves and a clever fox among dogs…**Become a lion to chase away wolves and become a fox to avoid traps.**

As a prisoner you must understand you are like a soldier, or an intelligence officer, trapped behind enemy lines. Everyone you must assume is your enemy or a potential threat. You must blend in, become invisible, evade, draw little attention, escape danger, and if necessary defend your life intelligently and fiercely. Psychologically you must mentally prepare yourself for all of these scenarios, and positive visualization exercise will help you prepare. Visualize yourself performing bravely, intelligently, and successfully in every possible situation. The more details you incorporate into your positive visualization exercise the more realistic it will become so that the mind will then see this and store it as an actual experience. Now when you find yourself in this situation 'for real' your mind will take on the memory of the experience you created, rather than panic, so you may react accordingly and more confidently...This is what we call Battle-Proofing the Mind.

Chapter 2.

AWARENESS, ADAPTATION,

AND

FABRICATING A POSITIVE ATTITUDE

The greatest tool/weapon a soldier, warrior, or prisoner possesses is the **human mind**. We've all heard the cliché, Mind Over Matter. Well the application of this in a survivalist situation is in one's awareness, adaptation, and fabricating a positive attitude using the power of the human mind…You **are** as you think.

Awareness not only refers to your powers of observation but also to the attention you pay to your 'intuition.' **Intuitive awareness,** often referred to as 'gut-instinct' or 'sixth sense', is when you **feel** something is not quite right. Or when you **feel** danger is in the air, or something just doesn't **feel** right. This level of awareness is very important in that it has saved the lives of many before you and will save you too if you listen to it and never second guess it. Many victims of misfortune or crime later say that they had a feeling something wasn't right but they thought it was just their paranoia, or they ignored it. This was their intuition subtly warning them of danger.

Always go with your gut instinct. If the television is sending you subliminal messages that the CIA is after you and to go out and hurt others, then you might be suffering from paranoid schizophrenia. Otherwise learn to trust in your intuitive feelings and go on your first instinct. To ignore it's warning may result in not living to regret it.

The most common form of awareness that comes to mind is our attention to the five senses: taste, touch, sound, smell, and sight. Common sense tells us if it smells or taste strange or bad do not eat it. This is part of our survival defense. If someone shakes our hand, or lays a hand on our shoulder, we can sense if they have bad or weird intention through our sense of touch. We often perceive most of our environment through the senses of sight and sound. And though we exercise these two senses, most of us do not train them to a high degree. Some people, such as cops, investigators, field intelligence officers, spies, elite military personnel, hunting scouts, and certain types of criminals, develop these senses to a high degree.

The field of surveillance/ counter-surveillance is a wide scope of information and techniques that would require an entire book of it's own, however, we will briefly go over some things you need to know in order to attune your awareness level to a higher degree and increase your survivability chances in prison or anywhere.

Stay Alert-Stay Alive, is a phrase repeated very often to military personnel and is a brother to the military phrase repeated equally as often, **'Pay Attention to Detail!'** In prison, just like in any other combat zone, you may learn to expect long periods of boredom followed by short periods of terror. And you must remain always alert if you want to stay alive. Prison is a concrete jungle, and being in a jungle one must never get too comfortable or lulled metaphorically to sleep. The smallest minute details unnoticed can mean death or injury. In the jungle loud noise is not 'usually' a sign of danger, but rather unusual silence is. Pay attention to any break in the rhythm of your environment. A sudden increase in noise volume, or a sudden decrease in noise volume, can imply danger. But silence always means the predators are about to strike. Silence in prison, just like in the jungle, means danger. That is your signal to exit the immediate area or, if you can not leave, get your back to a wall and stay out of the way.

Paying attention to small details, like a guy wearing gloves or thick clothing on a warm day usually means danger. Guys wearing gloves indoors or suddenly people moving away from you, maybe also watching you. If an attack is known to be going down, or an individual is marked, others will not want to be 'too' near him but everyone will be watching subtly because they want to see what goes down. An individual, or group of individuals, wearing what looks to be padding under their shirts, towels around the neck, and maybe ace bandages around the forearms, means they're dressed for war. You want to get out of the way, and hopefully get to your cell or a safer place. An individual or a few individuals migrating slowly to a part of the prison, chow hall, or yard, where they don't belong or seldom traffic is an alarm. An individual bending down to tie a shoe may be just doing that, or may be retrieving a weapon. A towel over a hand, a hand under a shirt or held low behind a leg, may be concealing a weapon. An individual walking around holding a cup of coffee or hot tea maybe doing that or may be carrying a cup of boiled water and magic-shave to scald someone in the face, so it's vital to one's survival to pay attention to detail and stay alert-stay alive.

In prison staring directly at others can be a hazard so learn to use a few surveillance/counter-surveillance techniques. Use reflective surfaces to see beside and behind you. A shadow on the ground can alert you to someone's approach from your rear. Wearing dark sunglasses can allow you to slightly turn your head in one direction while cutting your eyes over or upward in another direction. Pretending to be in deep thought and looking past your target while observing with your peripheral vision and then shifting your gaze elsewhere as if daydreaming. Glancing at objects above or near your target of observation allows you a pretext for observing them peripherally, but don't try it more than once, if they noticed, and keep your vision always roving. Practice using your eyes like a camera and take quick snap-shots, then in your mind's eye study the mental pictures and analyze them. With practice this technique will get easier and your powers of observation will improve. Scars, tattoos, calloused knuckles, limps, mannerisms, all tell a story about the individual. Also be aware of who socializes with whom: **Birds of a feather always flock together.** And in prison, politics is deadly serious. It's wise to know who and what an individual is, but also whom their allies are. Gangs, criminal organizations, and religious groups have their own greetings, handshakes, and rhetoric. This factor elevates the individual to part of a larger entity. An affront to the individual is an affront to the whole group. Their egos and pride is enormous and, being so, very delicate.

Adaptation is part of survival and nature illustrates the creatures which survive best are the ones who adapt more readily. This does not mean that you should become like the people you're now surrounded with. It's more of becoming quickly accustomed to your new surroundings and adjusting to your environment in a way that can function as a rational minded human being and maintain the undying will to prevail over 'come-what-may'. The tree that does not bend is easily broken. Therefore it's important to wear a mask to appease the masses. Giving respect to them who believe that respect is due to them. You are in 'their' world now and they want you to know it.

The guards, the wardens, and the gang entities have the power of numbers and brute force. You have the power of your mind and no one can break into or intrude upon it unless you give them the keys. Learn the written (and unwritten) rules of prison as soon as possible and adapt to them. They are there for your safety and survival. You don't have to respect anyone in your heart, but let them believe that you do. You bend to the storm, like bamboo, and when it passes you spring back upright. True strength requires flexibility of mind and body. This is a survival tactic one must adapt when surrounded by enemies and it is necessary to play the humble role. A trained covert operator, under cover, deep behind enemy lines, may have to pose as an unarmed journalist or red cross worker. Though he may be a SEAL Team member, a Delta Operator, a Special Forces soldier, or N.O.C. for the CIA, being outnumbered and surrounded by danger makes it necessary to adapt and blend in to your environment; to wear a mask to appease their egos and hide from them the truth. By doing so you will feel the power you take back over your life by fooling your enemies and your captors. Play to their delicate egos. And pity them.

Finally, in adapting to your environment, it is important to adapt to a daily routine. A routine will help channel the mind on other things besides the outside world and things you have no control over. Cleaning your cell, making your bunk, personal hygiene, exercise, reading, writing, studying, fighting your case, prayer, meditation, and a prison job or program participation. Try to keep as much of your day filled with activity, for the betterment of yourself, as possible.

Positive attitude is vitally important to surviving 'any' difficult or extraneous situation. For prisoners of war, or for cancer patients, a positive attitude can be the difference between life or death. It will be impossible to maintain something that does not exist, so this is why we say 'fabricating a positive attitude.' You've heard the saying, "Fake it until you make it." Well you can fabricate a positive attitude by self-indoctrination. It's similar to how the military indoctrinates soldiers by having them repeat self-affirmations and positive reinforcements until they start to believe it. When you find yourself thinking or mumbling negative reinforcements like, "I hate this place, I hate life, I'm sick of this world," consciously force yourself to counter with an opposite reinforcement. You don't need to like it or believe it, but if you repeat something enough it's proven that you will eventually believe it in your subconscious. And that will create a change overtime in your attitude. The military has used this with great effect, as have cults and the music industry, to fabricate a desired attitude. Combined with your battle-proofing techniques it becomes more effective in fabricating a positive attitude.

Here are a few positive counter-affirmations, some used by elite Military units, to fabricate a more positive and motivated attitude to facilitate the survivability and forging of the individual in times of extreme hardship and stress. You may adopt any of these affirmations, mantras, or create your own: "Pain and misery are a warrior's constant companions.

They will never leave you, nor forsake you, even when everyone else does. So open your arms and embrace them."…"The only easy day is yesterday."…"I like it here-I love it here."…"Pain and misery are my best friends."…"Hell is home for me now, but I will not break."…"I will bend but I do not break."…"Whatever doesn't kill me only makes me stronger."…"They can lock up my body but they can never lock up my mind."…"Strength and weakness both reside in the mind."…"Opposition only leads me to strong resolution."…"Mind over matter-If I don't mind-It don't matter."…"With every great difficulty comes a moment of relief."…"I walk between the raindrops and don't get wet."…"I am seeking peace within chaos."…"It could always be worse so it's not that bad."

It also goes far in fabricating a positive attitude to study books of comfort, encouragement, and faith. Chicken Soup for the Soul books are excellent reading for encouragement and inspiration. Tibetan Buddhism based books offer some psychological tools for stress management and calming the mind.

The books of Proverbs, Ecclesiastes, and the books of the New Testament, in the King James or Reina Valera Translation Holy Bible offer practical wisdom and comfort to many people. Remember, you reap what you sow. Or as they say in computer programming, "Garbage in-Garbage out." If you feed upon only the negative you will feel terrible all the time and your spirit will remain low. By force-feeding yourself positive thoughts, affirmations, reading material, and imaginations, you will (over time) retrain your mind to always look for the positive in even the worst situations. Two dogs live inside of us all and they're always fighting. One is positive (good) and one is negative (bad), and the one that we feed the most is the one that will win. It is a conscience effort to re-enforce the mind with positive counter-affirmations when all around you is only negative and evil. If the mind is the battlefield than you must become a proactive warrior and counter every negativity with a positive, and then follow through with a counter offensive of positive reinforcements and counter-affirmations in an attempt to overwhelm the negative attacks upon the mind.

Perception is a major tool in fabricating a positive attitude in a harsh and unforgiving environment. We all have developed our own perceptions over time and this perception is the mold that forms our attitude. Is the glass half full or half empty? Most individuals in prison, as in everyday life, tend to always see the glass half empty. Perhaps it stems from our desire for, or expectation of, a certain standard in life we have set or feel we should have. It is said that the rich person is the one who can find contentment in whatsoever situation that they find themselves. But how? It is a discipline of retraining the mind through conscious effort. Much how we retrain our muscles or even retrain a dog. It is by repetitive positive-counter-affirmation and discipline.

In the way of perception one may say, "I am in prison." Or one may change that perception and say, "I am in a monastery." You may see it as though you are a prisoner being held captive in a debasing dungeon of vile evil and filth. Or you may choose to exercise the power of positive counter-affirmation and see it as though you are actually in an institute of higher learning and physical training, which it can be if you choose it to be. You may choose to use the power of perception and see it anyway you choose, if it allows you to view your situation in a more positive light. The difference in the great successes, and heroic survivors, verses the defeated and miserable, is that the previous tend to adopt a more positive perception and counter the negative with positive counter-affirmations which contribute to a stronger will to prevail and a stronger spirit. Not to mention it contributes to better overall physical and mental health, which promotes greater survivability and overall well being.

This is not to say you will no longer ride the emotional and psychological roller-coaster of life's ups and downs. But you can create the change needed to escape remaining down and use perception to see the hard times as a time to grow and become stronger. A fine steel blade can only be forged by heat and pressure followed by cooling. A beautiful hard diamond is created only by heat and pressure over time. Then it is shaped and polished to become a fine jewel of great value for it's beauty, strength, and ability to reflect light. So it is with human beings. All growth and strength is preceded by times of hardship and pain. Comfort and pleasure are never conducive to physical, mental, emotional, or spiritual growth and training. As a survivor you must adopt the mentality of a warrior/ scholar. Everything is merely a test to strengthen you or make you wiser.

Everything is a test in this world. In time you will look back at your most difficult moments in life with some feeling of pride that you endured with fortitude and survived. You might even grow to appreciate the hardships and trials that forged you into a stronger and wiser person of character. We often grow into mature beings not despite the manure of our lives but rather, like a beautiful rich garden or strong tree, because of it.

Furthermore, after all of the techniques and tricks discussed here for retraining the mind and fabricating a positive attitude, we should address the issue of personal faith and positive effect it has in the attitude of many who live in terrible conditions. The fact is that anyone who is logical, or has studied creation with serious objectivity, can not deny the existence of a Creator or Supreme Being commonly referred to as God. And most of us have a conscience and when we violate that conscience we feel self-condemnation (guilt) and inwardly feel a desire to be forgiven. Where does this moral conscience come from, and why do all people across the globe seek to appease or make peace with a deity or god? Where does our morality come from? We are all innately judges, judging ourselves and others. When see a child or helpless person being abused most of us feel angry. When a stranger hurts our loved ones we feel angry and desire retribution. When someone steals from us we condemn their actions as a violation of some moral law or rule.

.

By condemning those who have done us, our loved ones, wrong we declare that there is a universal right and wrong. And when we ourselves do dirt, or do wrong, our inner being convicts us by the same standards that we hold others to. Also, most peoples throughout the world feel a desire to seek and know their Creator, and we feel a need to call out to someone in prayer during times of desperation. Sometimes we get angry and hold resentment toward our Creator (or God) when tragedy strikes or we feel our prayers were not answered. But as human beings we naturally seek comfort in our faith, or faith in 'something'. We need to believe in something because it gives up hope and strength. Faith is important to survival and a positive attitude. So cultivate your faith and maintain (or find) hope in **something,** because an individual without hope is already dead.

In the end your personal survival skills may be summarized by a Positive Attitude, Heightened Awareness, and Adapt & Overcome.

Chapter 3.

ENDURING HARDSHIP

AND

SUFFERING.

Here we will cover the topic of enduring hardships and discuss some techniques you may learn to use and apply to any situation of hardship or suffering. Some military schools and government agencies train personel to use the very techniques that will be discussed here in enduring hardship and suffering. You may find yourself shackled, cuffed, packed onto an old bus with no ventilation, a backed-up toilet creating nausea and headache from the ammonia and methane, perhaps the vehicle exhaust is leaking into the compartment, and you're sitting on a very hard seat with no knee room surrounded by loud barking men who smell like wet livestock. Or you may find yourself in the 'hole' (isolation unit) on a concrete block bunk, in a paper-gown, no clothing or blanket, no sleeping mat, in filthy surroundings, and the air blowing from the vent into your cell is freezing like a walk in cooler. It sounds inhumane and it is probably unconstitutional, but there is a very good chance you could find yourself in similar circumstances to what I've just described here (or worse). There are places all over the country and across the globe where prisoners, detainees, and patients find themselves in some extreme hardships. We often think that in the United

States prisoners have rights to protect them from inhumane treatment and torturous conditions, but it happens every single day. You may find yourself forced to suffer with inguinal hernias for six years before prison medical finally agrees to send you for surgery. Only after you have filed a 1983 Civil Action against the warden and everyone whom is responsible for your care, for violation of your 8th Amendment right under the U.S. Constitution. You may find yourself forced to live several months with an abscess tooth, or endure a torn ACL in your knee for years, due to deliberate indifference to a serious medical need. I pray that you never have to endure anything so hard during your time in our gated-community, but proper preparation prevents poor performance and here you'll find valuable tools to aid one who finds their self in times of enduring hardship and suffering.

Anyone whom has had the displeasure of surviving the U.S. Army S.E.R.E. program (survival, evasion, resistance, escape) or interrogation/ counter-interrogation and counter-detention training will be familiar with some or most of these concepts. The advantage that they had during these programs is that, no matter how unpleasant it got, there was the comforting realization in the back of one's mind that there was an end to it all in the not so distant future. For the individual who may be suffering and enduring extreme hardships in a prison setting and is doing anywhere from 25yrs to 'Life' without parole that individual does not have the luxury of such comforting knowledge. So we must take that into consideration and modify our whole approach to a more indefinite time period. We know there will not be a rescue team coming to get us, or anyone negotiating politically for our release, and our chances of escape & evasion are slim to none. Our only hope is in the Courts and in answered prayers. But here are some serious tools to aid anyone with enduring hardship and suffering, be they a p.o.w., a prisoner of the state, federal prisoner, or being held anywhere against one's will.

      COMPARTMENTALIZATION, refers to separating everything in your life mentally into it's own separate mental compartment. This prevents personal problems, family problems, legal problems. professional problems, etc. from compounding and overwhelming you. People have nervous breakdowns and snap because they become overwhelmed by too much compounding upon their mind. So we develop this technique of compartmentalization to allow ourselves to mentally handle the pressures of stress and reduce our suffering. Pressure busts pipes and too much pressure overtime will induce mental breakdown and physical pains and illness. So we must use a technique that allows us to reduce the psychological work load. Imagine the stress of all of your work, bills, legal papers, letters (etc.) all piled up in a disorganized clutter on top of your desk and you have to work with this mess daily. The only logical and intelligent thing to do is create a filing system where each topic has it's own compartment where you can take it out and address it when needed and store it away before addressing a different topic. Picture your mind as a place full of filing compartments where you can compartmentalize every part of your life into it's own separate compartment. Some create in their mind doors to separate rooms where a different part of your life resides. One then may open and close the appropriate door when needed and address or dismiss whichever part of one's life when needed. As a prisoner you will find it extremely vital to compartmentalize your outside life from your prison existence. You will need to compartmentalize your family and emotions from your survival situation at hand. Place all of your deep emotions, love, and desire for your love ones into a special box or room in your mind and lock it with a golden key. Now create for yourself another room, or compartment, and place within it all of your best & most special memories. This is your special place, and you can secretly go there to escape whenever needed. Now create a compartment for your legal case, one for your exercise/training routine, one for your job or program, and so-on-forth. This technique is taught to elite military personnel, government agents, fortune 500 executives, politicians, and many professionals who deal with an eclectic overwhelming amount of issues each day and it is very effective and useful in the realm of counter-incarceration (surviving prison.)

FOCUS-WITHIN, refers to redirecting one's focus from the circumstances and environmental hardship, at that particular time in which you have not the power to change it, and redirecting one's focus inward. It's one form of exercising psychological detachment by removing the self from an unpleasant or very harsh physical environment in which you can not physically escape and are forced to endure. In the military we often use the phrase, "Separate the mind from the body." This is a very ancient technique practiced by warriors since perhaps time began. Focus within and withdraw the mind from the body so that the mind acts now more like an observer during time of hardship and suffering than as an actual participant. Long distance runners often employ a similar technique to endure the hardship and suffering of their endurance test.

An alternative technique is to mentally rise above your self. To detach by stepping outside of yourself and watching yourself, your environment, and your suffering from almost a third person perspective. Not as the one experiencing the hardship and suffering but as a detached observer, separating your mind from your body.

RETURN-TO-THE-BREATH, entails returning to your Combat-Breathing exercise during moments of hardship and suffering. This goes far in reducing stress and pain during moments of hardship and suffering. This goes far in reducing stress and pain during moments of hardship and suffering. This aids in the reduction of stress and pain both physically and mentally. You will direct your focus on the breath as discussed earlier in chapter one's battle-proofing the mind. Inhale four seconds through the nostrils and exhale six seconds out of the mouth. In 4: Out 6. Follow the breath by emptying your mind and placing all of your attention on the breath. As pain, discomfort, worries, stress, anger, and regret come to torment your mind, heart, and body just detach and return to the breath. Let everything go and focus only on the breath. Like an ocean tide rolling in and gently rolling back out. All thoughts are just clouds drifting past. All suffering, hardship, and pain are just clouds passing by and you're not grasping to hold onto them. Just let them pass on by and focus completely on the tide of the calm, gentle, breath. Inhale four and exhale six...return to the breath...follow the breath.

MAINTAIN FAITH & HOPE WITH YOUR HIGHER POWER. If you do not have faith in a Creator, in God, than find what you do believe and hope in. 'Faith' is complete trust. 'Hope' is a desire for something with confident expectation. 'Trust' is complete reliance in the integrity or ability of someone or something. Mental techniques, breathing exercises, battle proofing the mind, and positive counter-reinforcements will go far in providing you with effective counter-incarceration tools. But they will take you only so far...It's vital that you maintain faith and hope in whatever or whomever you have absolute and total trust.

Personally, for me, after years of soul searching, studying all the world's major religions (and a few minor ones). And practicing native spirituality and shaman medicine, I found the truth to be in the Creator, Lord Jesus (Y'e'shua) Christ, after many supernatural experiences and miracles along my journey. But whether you have complete faith and hope in God, Allah, Brahma, Krishna, Buddha, Dao, Mithra, Jah, Law of Attraction, or the tooth fairy, you **need** faith and hope in your life. It will give you what you need to endure long term hopelessness, despair, hardship, and suffering. Without hope, one is like a ship without sails or rudder, cast upon a terrible sea of despair.

We are unremarkably and fearfully designed beings living in a universe of mysteries, upon an earth of great wonders. To study nature, biology, and anatomy is to become aware of the awesome engineering, design, and incomprehensible intelligence of a divine Creator. A big explosion and random chance can not design and build a sophisticated Lexus SC430. You study the intricate design and craftsmanship and you know it originated from an intelligent designer & Creator.

Find your faith and hope, than hold onto it. **In prison you must nurture the hope that there is still hope.**

Chapter 4.

CONCRETE JUNGLE

AND

UNWRITTEN RULES.

It is said that prison is a concrete jungle and in many ways this is so. Like a jungle it is full of predators, scavengers, chameleons, and parasites. And also like the jungle, every moment is about survival. Some try to survive by being invisible and quiet, so as not to draw attention to their self. This may work for awhile, but eventually predators will take notice and then hiding in plain site will not work anymore as a sole method of survival. Some will become chameleons, much like a politician, and try to win the hearts and minds of everyone around by becoming a mirror that reflects back to them their self. Since most people are narcissistic at heart this technique is often very effective for some people. 'Predators' usually run in packs, though there are some exceptions, because in a pack they have safety and strength in numbers. No different than coyotes, dogs, hyenas, and chimps. 'Parasites' often survive by feeding on everyone around them, and receive some protection by association. Sometimes a parasite can also be a chameleon or a predator, but not as a rule. 'Prey' are just that, as the word implies. To be succinct we will just say that there are three groups of individuals in the concrete jungle-Predators, Prey, and Survivors. (It is better to be the survivor.)

In the concrete jungle you soon notice that nothing is normal anymore, and you may feel you've fallen down the proverbial rabbit hole and ended up in an alternate universe. Just try to remember nothing is really as it seems. The loud, rough looking, guy may be a cowardly lion living in fear so he compensates by being loud, talking mean, and looking rough. The quiet, humble, educated convict may be a vicious wolf in sheep's clothing. So you must believe nothing you hear and only half of what you see. You're in the jungle now so keep your mouth shut, your ears open, and D.T.A. (Don't Trust Anyone). Even the correctional officers are not to be trusted. Many are dirty and treacherous. Few are solid.

You may not know it now but there are correctional officers, case managers, and even assistant wardens, and prison medical personnel who are associated (if not affiliated) with criminal organizations or members of criminal organizations. And prison administration gossip as much, if not more, than the convicts. So, D.T.A..

It's in the best interest of prison officials to act as instigators, and keep stuff stirred up between the prison population, because as long as they keep the prisoners fighting and killing each other then the administration feels safer. What they fear is 'unity' and comradery among the prison population as a whole. Because then they, the administration, may become the common enemy and target of every subgroup within the entire prison population. So just as the Roman empire, and later the British empire, they encourage some level of inner turmoil and paranoia among the prisoners to ensure their own safety and seat of authority. It's called, the divide and conquer strategy. So do not assume they are there with your best interest at heart, or 'your' safety as their main concern.

Prison is full of snitches, or confidential informants, but it's not in your best interest to engage in this type of activity, for the simple fact that the officers you give information to may be in business with the individual (or individuals) you're snitching on. You never know, so don't risk your life…Remain low key.

If you feel a moral obligation to report someone being abused by sexual predators, the safest method is to mail an in-house letter (anonymously) to the chief of security and write it in your non-dominate hand to disguise your handwriting. Make sure the administration, nor the prisoners, can trace this letter to you. Your safety is at stake.

It is best if you do not participate in sports or ballgames in the penitentiary. Not only do you risk a serious violent altercation when playing competitive sports with violent individuals in prison, but any accidental injury is likely to go untreated. You want to avoid mechanical injury in prison. Medical care is the bare minimum, if you even get that. Broken bones are often just wrapped with an ace bandage and never reset. A broken tooth, if it causes pain, will just be pulled rather than salvaged and possibly repaired. Torn ligaments, snapped tendons, detached muscles, herniated disc, and inguinal hernias will go untreated for years (or indefinitely).

It's safer and more prudent to create your own exercise regimen of walking, jogging, stretching, and calisthenics to maintain health, fitness, and reduce stress. Avoid prison sports and competitive games.

It's wise to avoid card games or competitive games of any kind. But once you're established and maybe know an individual for some years you may be able to engage that particular individual in a quiet game of chess, dominoes, or cards if there is no wagering involved. Violence can erupt from the simplest friendly game.

Maintain strict personal hygiene to eliminate health risks, painful cavities or abscesses, which often go untreated for long periods of time, and the risk of offending prisoners who live in close proximity to you. Violence can erupt over a cell mate who refuses to maintain hygiene and carries an offensive odor. Keep your bedding and laundry clean and you'll get along better with others. Keep your sink and toilet jack clean after each time you use it. And dry out the sink after use.

When defecating in your cell flush as you drop if the toilet allows multiple flushes. Some prisons have incorporated a flush governor on the toilets limiting the number of flushes per hour or so. Also, as a courtesy if you have some baby powder or can acquire some through the prison commissary puff a little in the air after a number two visit. Show respect and some level of consideration to your cell mates (cellees) and you're more likely to be given the same.

Hide your smiles and cries. Both are a sign of weakness in prison and beware of 'anyone' who smiles at you. Con-men, predators, and sexual-predators tend to use smiles to disarm a new fish. So be on alert when anyone smiles at you in the concrete jungle. Remember, in the animal kingdom baring one's teeth is a sign of aggression. Also, crying is weakness and the predators live to hunt the weak. Perhaps your personal belief is that a real man can shed tears, but you're in a new world now. Hide your smiles and cries and keep your personal business personal. No one cares about your personal business unless they are a con man or predator trying to win your trust. Tell **no one** about your family, where they work, where they live, or their names. (Don't Trust Anyone.) All personal mail from your family, friends, and loved ones, should have the return address immediately torn off the envelope upon receipt and torn up and flushed. You may want to chew it up and flush it. A great deal of damage can be done through someone acquiring an address or phone number of your people. Extortion, fraud, terrorism, and stalking are just a 'few' minor examples.

Any of your legal paperwork, documents, or sentence of judgment orders, may contain your social security number. Black this out immediately, because it's a common way prisoners will get your S.S.N. and steal your identity. Don't worry about damaging the document because the criminal courts **will** accept any copies you have to submit with your appeals, or habeas corpus, later on without your S.S.N.

You will hear some new words you've never heard before and many old words with new meanings in prison culture. A 'boy', punk, gump, sissy, mariposo (not mariposa) jotito and homosexual are one in the same. These words refer to a feminine homosexual, or also a sex slave forced to provide services to a predator or group of predators. Many sexual predators in prison who participate in homosexual acts with a 'punk', or take by force another prisoner's body and dignity, do not consider themselves to be homosexuals in the least sense. Many have wives, significant others, and children who visit them. Many are attracted to the opposite sex, but they just have sex with the same gender in prison and justify it through twisted reasoning. If one were to accuse them of homosexuality they would be highly offended and may become aggressive. Do not try to understand this strange illogical reasoning for there is very little that is logical in the concrete jungle. The fact remains, whether pitching or catching they're still playing ball for the same team. These individuals are very dangerous and irrational, so do your best to avoid them anyway you can.

A 'duck' is similar to a 'mark', or a victim. This refers to someone who is naïve, gullible, or easy to take advantage of. Someone who is generous, or easy to fleece, is a 'duck'. Kindness is perceived as weakness by many in prison.

A 'crash-dummy' is usually a young individual that can be

manipulated to crash-out or left to their own devices will crash-out on their own. They will pull a stunt and go to maximum security with little encouragement. They will stab another prisoner or a guard in front of witnesses. They just don't care about anything so they're reckless and foolish. Prison gangs will use a crash dummy as a 'send-out'. Old cons will manipulate a crash-dummy to do their dirty work for them. A 'send-out' is someone used to carry out someone else's dirty work and they're expendable. A send out is usually either young, naïve, foolish, desires to be accepted, or wants to prove themselves and earn respect from their peers any way possible. They are easily seduced and manipulated by the subtle minded puppeteer. Gangs love send-outs.

A 'mule' is one who carries or transports drugs, weapons, cell phones, tattoo paraphernalia on (or in) their person for others. Dope packages, cell phones, shanks, lock blade knives and tattoo guns are **all** carried inside the rectal cavity of some individuals in prison. A mule may work by choice or by force of threat.

A 'butcher', shank, shiv, 'thang', bone crusher, W.M.D., pica, fiero or strap all refer to a weapon used to stab or open up another individual. It maybe an ice pick, blade, or a dagger. And often are tipped with poison, feces, or even HIV/ hepatitis infected blood.

A 'booty-bandit', head-hunter, bull-queer, or 'wolf', refers to sexual predators within the prison system whom prey upon other prisoners. A 'daddy' or boy-chaser refers to an individual who maintains or seeks relationships with a young man or a homosexual punk.

A 'snitch', C.I. (confidential informant), rat, sapo, dedo, or chismoso is one who gives information, or is seen talking, to the administration or police. 'Police' refers to anyone working for law enforcement or the penal system. Also 'police' may refer to a snitch.

A 'chi-mo', chicken hawk, chester, or baby-raper refers to individuals who prey on children sexually. They are the most hated individuals in prison, whether they're guilty or wrongfully convicted, and are the target of predators and prison gangs.

'Dog' is a term used by specific gangs to greet one another. Usually this is a term used by the Bloods criminal gang. 'Cuz' is a term used by Crip gang members to greet one another. I/E: What's crackin cuz? 'Kinfolk' is a term usually used by Gangster Disciples to greet each other.

This is only a very short list of words you will hear often in prison and need to know the meanings of for personal awareness. There are 'many' more, but one would have to create a dictionary to include them all. Here we want to give you some trigger words so that one will not say the wrong thing while also understanding what may be said around or directly to you.

Maybe you've heard the expression, "Birds of a feather flock together." This is true, but nowhere is it more so than here in the prison system. You will be expected to, and it would behoove you to, socialize with your own. If your racially mixed then you will be expected to drift to the racial group you look most like. Your grandma maybe a Cherokee, like many claim, but if **you** look like an Anglo Saxon you're 'white'. If you look to be an African American than you are considered to be 'black'. If you're Hispanic or Native American Indian you will stick with others who look like you. Asians stick together and are often accepted within the Hispanic/Native American community in prison. To hang out with, work out with, or sit at chow with a different racial group is trouble within the concrete jungle. It is a sad reality but in prison Caucasians with Caucasians, Blacks with Blacks, and Hispanic/ Native American with Hispanics. Asians with other Asians or often with Hispanics. It is prison survival and one of the unwritten rules of the concrete jungle. You have to remember you're not in the free world anymore. Now within the racial divide there are further subgroups within and outside of this spectrum. Gangs, criminal organizations, religious groups/cults, etc... And then individuals of a like mind tend to group together.

In the concrete jungle you are known by the company that you keep and they believe birds of a feather flock together. Regardless of your charge or character, if one hangs out with homosexuals one is a homosexual. If one hangs out with tree-jumpers (rapists) one is viewed as a rapist. If one hangs out with a gang or criminal organization one will be seen as one of them by other prisoners and the prison administration. So do not be surprised if your prison file says you're a suspected security threat group member. And the parole board will consider any and everything the administration puts in your file should you ever go up. If you socialize with sex offenders of any kind, or with punks, you will be marked as one of them and it will be a stain on your reputation from then on. And the wolves will try to move on you the first chance they get. (Birds of a feather flock together.)

It's also important that you learn the different gangs and organizations as well as observe who is affiliated or associated with which group. Not all gang members are tattooed, or marked, with their gang 'patch'. Some are called 'sleepers' and are deliberately unmarked so that they may go undetected and act as intelligence gatherers. So observing who socializes with whom and what circles they move in is key to one's survival, as we've mentioned several times for emphasis, "birds of a feather flock together." If you cell with someone it's important to know what they're part of and who has their back.

D.T.A…Don't trust anyone. Prison is very much like being inside of a deadly spy novel where nothing is quite as it may seem and everyone is either an enemy agent, or a double agent, while your closest friend is your worst enemy. So it's important to stay alert, maintain your health the best as one can, stay fighting fit, remain security-conscience, do **not** trust anyone, listen much but speak very little. The less people you speak to the better off you will be in the concrete jungle.

There are many unwritten rules for doing time with as few problems as possible. Learn these rules and they may save your life and keep you out of trouble. Most prisoners who are new to the system; fresh fish, have to learn these things the hard way. Some learn them the **very** hard way. So now we will go over the 'unwritten rules' (in writing). Some we've already discussed, but that's okay because life and death hang upon whether one learns these rules and lives by them. It's my hope that they will save someone's life and contribute to peace and harmony within one's time building in the concrete jungle known as 'prison'. (Don't learn the hard way!)

1. D.T.A. (Don't Trust Anyone.) This is the most important rule.
2. Stay Alert; Stay Alive. Keep your eyes and ears open and your mouth closed.
3. Treat everyone with respect. Prisoners and Administration. If you want to receive respect you first have to give respect. It's the law of reciprocity. And it **is** law.
4. Repeat no gossip and never engage in any backbiting of **any** kind.
5. Mind your own business and do your own time.
6. Stick with your own kind and let no one abuse your people unjustly.
7. Don't socialize with, or suck up to, the administration. Let them do their job and you do your time. No fraternizing with the 'police.'
8. Believe nothing you hear and only half of what you see.
9. Never back down and let **no one** abuse you. Stand up for yourself always.
10. If you bump into someone, or they bump into you, politely say excuse me. Don't worry if it be their fault or yours.
11. Be mentally prepared to kill or die at any moment.
12. Hide your smiles and your cries.
13. Keep your personal problems personal. No one wants to hear it.
14. Keep your living space clean and clean up after yourself.
15. Never sleep with cell door open or unsecure. Sit on **no one's** bunk but your own.
16. Let no one take 'anything' from you. If they can take something small without a fight then they will go after other things.
17. Don't spit in the sink. Spit in the toilet-jack when you brush your teeth.
18. Destroy the return address on letters from family and love ones immediately upon receipt.
19. Never discuss your love one's names, jobs, schools, or location with **anyone.**

20. Never ask anyone about their charge.
21. Never leave your cell wearing only shower shoes or house shoes, but keep your boots or sneakers on for traction in case of an attack.
22. Don't engage in snitching of any kind.
23. Pay your debts, no matter how small, and be on time with it.
24. Take your own charges. If you get a disciplinary or write up don't expect someone else to take your charge or to cop to 'your' contraband.
25. Don't interfere with anyone else's hustle.
26. Never Assume Anything.
27. Expect the Unexpected.
28. Maintain your personal hygiene.
29. Exercise to stay physically and mentally fit & reduce stress.
30. Never cut in line. You wait your turn.
31. Call no one outside their name, or the name they go by. And let no one call you outside of yours.
32. Except no gifts. **Nothing** is ever free in the concrete jungle!

We should reiterate that one is known by the company they keep. A Chinese proverb says, "Show me who you walk with and I'll tell you who you are." Keep this in mind always. It will effect how you are perceived and how you will perceive others.

In the concrete jungle 99.9% of individuals are out to get 'something' from you someway or another. Some use clever seduction, manipulation, deception, intimidation, and naked aggression. But the one who pretends to want nothing deserves the most scrutiny. Everyone wants to use you and everyone wants 'something'. Nobody is your true friend in prison, except God, and nothing is ever free. To believe different is at one's own peril.

As a fresh fish, or new prisoner, one will be tested most certainly by an individual or individuals. They call it a 'heart check'. I must advise strongly, do not back down! Even if they have knives! You must get aggressive and turn fear into an ally and fight like a vicious lion if you have to. The moment you feel an attack is imminent go on the offense and make the element of surprise your own advantage. If you do not already have a life sentence it would behoove you not to earn one by taking a life in prison if it's unavoidable. It is often sufficient to fight and injure or neutralize a threat without killing anyone. If you fight and earn your respect, do so with humility. Never brag, or you may incite someone you fought or their allies to make an example of you and maim, cripple, or kill you. (Or worse.) If you get the best of someone in a fight, never talk about it or strut around like a tough guy. They may feel the need to exact revenge and arrogance maybe the provocation needed to act on it in order to save face.

Never underestimate 'anyone'. Never judge a book by its cover or it could cost you your life. The smallest, most feminine, tinker bell maybe a cold blooded killer. Often the smaller the individual is the more violent. It's called the Napoleonic Complex in psychology when smaller individuals, due to insecurity, overcompensate for their lack of physical stature by being more violent tempered and aggressive. It's also true in prison what is often said about the quiet ones, as well as the ones in contrast who smile a lot and seem strangely cheerful all of the time. They are more dangerous than the ones who talk loudly, barking a lot and acting hard. Like dogs, in prison the ones that bark a lot and often talk tough are usually scared. The seasoned predators know this and are not fooled. But the dog that appears quiet and brooding is often the one that will attack.

In the concrete jungle there are lots of tough individuals and killers are a dime for a dozen. No one is intimidated by the tough. Rather it's the crazy one that they watch out for. The crazy one is unpredictable and therefore seemingly more volatile. The quiet, brooding, and crazy individual is less of a target to the predators. However, if people fear that individual 'too much' they will find a way to eliminate that threat because there are those who will not live in constant fear. So it's somewhat complicated.

Let me clarify how we use the word 'crazy'. In prison majority of the population are a walking textbook psychosis. It would appear at first glance that everyone is crazy, or an outright lunatic, so who are the 'crazy ones' that prisoners consider as being dangerously crazy? Well, the individual that tries to **act** crazy will be recognized at once and draw too much attention to their self. In prison most people are social creatures and the extremely anti-social is the first sign of crazy. Someone who has conversations with themselves when they think no one's paying attention, who stares off into nowhere and appears to be seeing into another world, who's behavior is subtly sociopathic and who has an unblinking, bright, stare in their eyes, but seldom make eye contact with humans unless spoken to...Basically, someone who lives in another world altogether.

The 'crazy' ones are unpredictable and can (do) snap without any kind of warning. And they fight more viciously, like a wild animal, while feeling no pain. To go from calm to wildly violent and back to calm again is somewhat crazy in prison. Usually it's the quiet antisocial ones who live in their own world and exhibit no emotion in their eyes and face. Those are the ones who will go 'Hannibal Lector' and so they are usually left alone.

In time you will come to learn that many individuals doing time, even some of the administration, are bi-polar. One minute they're fine and stable, but without reason they can become angry or depressed. They're on an emotional roller coaster. They can go from talking your ear off like you're their best friend, to being withdrawn and throwing you dirty looks like you're their worst enemy. This is more common than you may think, so don't take it personal. Just give these individuals their space.

It may be hard for a social individual at first, but the less people you speak to in prison the better off you will be. So one must become somewhat antisocial and create a world to them selves. Some get lost in books, in writing, in their exercise and body building, or in their prayer life. Some do all of the above.

Like in the jungle silence is not a good sign. There's always a little silence before a storm. Before a large fight, a gang war, or a stabbing you may sense a hum of tension in the air. Sometimes it will get just a little bit more quiet than normal. That's when it's time to get out of the way, or get to your cell.

In prison, politics is a daily part of life and can be deadly. For many their safety and security hangs on their reputation. To attack or insult that reputation is perceived as an attack on their life and they may very well react violently in order to maintain their safety and security. One must guard their reputation with their life for it is their life that they are guarding. It is quite common in prison for adversaries to assassinate one's character in order to win support for their personal agenda while turning hearts and minds against you. This is often necessary to alienate the individual from any potential ally support, or sympathizers, and is done by propaganda or outright lying. It's a tactic drawn from Sun Tzu's **The Art of War** and used extensively in politics, business, warfare, and prison. Once they convince the prison population you are something as detestable as a baby raper, or a snitch, then they can physically attack you in whatever way they desire and it will appear justifiable to the masses. They've politically isolated you from sympathizers or allies by assassinating your character and fabricating a pretext to justify your harm.

One counter to this political strategy of character assassination is to subtly allow 'certain' individuals to see your charge in writing; I/E: time sheet or sentence of judgment form, while never fraternizing at all with prison authorities, pedophiles, or any homosexuals. Give your adversaries nothing to work with.

An old convict gave me this bit of advice when I first arrived in the concrete jungle. Matthew 10:16 from the King James translation of the holy bible; "Behold, I send you forth as sheep in the midst of wolves: be ye therefore wise as serpents, and pure as doves."

Chapter 5.

SELF-DEFENSE AND PHYSICAL TRAINING

Now we must address the issues of self-defense and physical training in prison. Which go hand-in-hand. Most readers will assume that self-defense refers to physical hand to hand combat. That is a small part of it, but here we will cover many other areas of self-defense. An ounce of prevention is always worth more than a ton of cure. So let's begin by covering the six parts of self-defense and some examples of their application to the prison environment.

WISDOM, which is sometimes defined as 'common sense or good judgment,' is the first rule of self-defense. Immediately following comes the second rule.

AVOIDANCE, as defined by the American Heritage Dictionary, is to stay clear of; evade; to keep from happening; prevent; to refrain from. In prison one may practice avoidance to a great degree by practicing the 'unwritten rule' laid out in the previous chapter, and observing a few new ones here. In prison one may practice avoidance to a great degree by practicing the 'unwritten rules' laid out in the previous chapter, and observing a few now ones here:

Don't gamble. Don't get into debt. Stay away from 'punks'. Show respect. Don't backbite or gossip. Don't play sports or competitive games of any kind. Show no fear or timidity. Don't trust anyone. Don't get into a gang (or organization). And don't mess with drugs, cell phones, or tobacco and prison alcohol (hooch).

Avoid isolated areas and blind spots. These are places where an attack is ideal for prison gangs and predators. Avoid areas where you'd be at a disadvantage against multiple attackers. And you want to avoid areas where you don't 'blend in', as well as gang congregation areas. This is difficult, but not impossible.

Avoid the arrogant, argumentative, and angry individual. Avoid the loud mouths and ones who seem to socialize with too many people. Avoid the ones who brood and sulk. Avoid conversation with others, but if you can not then do all of the listening and offer no real opinion. Pretend to understand and pretend to agree unless it clearly is against your morality. In that case simply shake your head and say, "I don't know about that." But be evasive and placate when engaged in conversation by cell mates. Wear a mask to appease the masses.

Avoid telling individuals what city, town, or even state your love ones live in. Use disinformation by deliberately misleading them when asked. Like wise when they ask where you're calling to on the phone give them a state far away, perhaps letting them know your people don't have 'three way' phone and can not afford to call long distance.

Avoid eye contact with others, but when confronted and it's necessary to make eye contact don't blink. Create a dead emotionless stare but don't try to stare hard, mean, or intimidate anyone. Make your face an emotionless mask and your eyes dead. If you need to blink, break eye contact. You wont be trying to intimidate anyone and create a situation, nor will you appear to be prey to the predators or intimidated by anyone. And remember to always hide your smiles and cries. Show no emotions to anyone. (Be stoic.)

Avoid offense and argument. The best defense, some say, is not to offend. Avoid situations, actions, and places conducive to potential altercation or violence of some sort. Use wisdom and practice avoidance.

De-escalation is 'to decrease the scope or intensity of.' This applies to verbal confrontations, arguments, and physical confrontation proceeding a violent altercation. This is a technique taught to military, law enforcement, and security personal, as well as to civilians in self-defense classes. It's a matter of common sense not to add fuel to a fire that can burn out of control. You must be the one to exercise self-discipline, control of your emotional responses, and sacrifice prideful ego by out thinking the fools and ego maniacs around you. Eighty percent or more of communication is thought to be nonverbal, so by your body language, facial expressions, and eyes you can escalate or de-escalate a situation by exhibiting certain emotions or thoughts.

Escalators can be exhibiting arrogance, condescension, aggression, anger, fear, timidness, or superiority.

De-escalators can be exhibiting strength, understanding, respect, Equality, calmness, rationality, neutrality, a non-threatening demeanor, and humble confidence.

Return to the breath. Focus on your breath and inhale through the nose and exhale out of the mouth, slow and steady breaths. By calming your breath, you calm the mind, which calms the emotion. By calming yourself and remaining calm you can better calm the situation, or at least not escalate it. Control your breath and control your emotion. There is a saying in the eastern martial arts: Breath is mind; Mind is breath.

Using the power of your sound and word to verbally de-escalate a situation is important. Not only must you carefully control the tone of your voice by keeping it calm, respectful, strong, understanding, and neutral, but your words must achieve the same desired effect. This requires gifted speech.

Gifted speech is important in de-escalating a situation. When speaking, weigh your words, consider your tone, and tailor your words for the individual to whom you are speaking. In speaking remember that less is more. Most people respond to rationality and respectfulness, but there are some in prison who do not.

To give an example for a better understanding, one might be confronted by an individual or group of individuals who seem to be looking for trouble or are being very disrespectful. One must almost consider this theater and so create a theatrical performance. Your opposition are merely characters in the same scene as you. One might say, "Sir if you want respect you must give respect. To have people fear is to have them hate and there is no respect where there is hate. To be respected is to be honored. We don't have to be friends. We don't have to even like each other. But I will never disrespect you, so don't disrespect me. This is the way of men." (This is just one possible example and what I've said with positive effects.) By combining calm, humble, strength with a respectful, non-threatening, demeanor one can deliver this speech with great affect. The power of life and death is in the words. So study the writings of great authors, the words of great speakers, and learn how to use words to influence the hearts and minds of those around you. Do not underestimate the power of sound and words. People have fought wars, sacrificed their lives, and gone to the grave for individuals who understood how to use words to influence the hearts and minds of others. Others have used words to talk down jumpers and defuse killers and terrorists.

Deterrence is to prevent or discourage from acting, as by means of fear or doubt. It is said power perceived is power achieved. A good mixture of humbleness and strength is a good deterrence. Do not be one of those individual who go to prison a start telling everyone they talk to they're a navy SEAL commando, Army infantry Ranger, or a third degree black belt in Israeli Krav Maga (even if it happens to be true) thinking you will deter gangs and prison predators. In fact you'll have quite the opposite affect that you desire. Either they'll perceive your fear as the reason you're trying to intimidate or deter anyone from messing with you, and this is like blood in the water to sharks when convicts and gangs smell fear, or, secondly, they will perceive you bragging as a personal challenge to every prison tough guy, killer, and gang. So don't draw attention to yourself by building a paper tiger and if you really are a trained human weapon don't make the mistake of tooting your horn. If you want a lot of prison drama being your own fight promoter and building up hype is sure to make your time in prison a very interesting one.

On the contrary, arouse no curiosity by appearing mysterious and do not show any weakness in your character or physical constitution. Appear humble, respectful, quiet, emotionless, strong and disinterested in other people's business. Make it a point to exercise daily and stay fighting fit. The nature of a predator is to prey upon the weak, timid, and gullible. So deterrence is to appear to be the exact opposite. By exercising physical fitness daily, with a degree of seriousness, you wont be in the weak category. Lifting massive weights doesn't make you fighting fit. It builds strength over time, if you manage to avoid an inguinal hernia, but it doesn't build endurance, stamina, cardio and speed. Calisthenics such as push-ups, fist-push ups, finger tip push-ups, tiger claw push-ups, wide arm push-ups, body dips, lunges, deep knee-bends, squat-thrusts, crunches, jumping jacks (side straddle hops) and jogging/running are the core set of exercises one needs to make part of their daily religion. These will strengthen, build, and condition the body properly so that one will be what we call 'Fighting Fit' and the wolves will be watching & observing, so a display of strength and fitness often is enough to deter them to hunt for weaker prey. However you may attract the eye of the gang recruiters and be invited to join their 'organization' in their own madness. *Respectfully* tell them it's against your personal, moral, and religious convictions and you don't believe in that path because your personal journey is taking you along a different path. Explain that you want to get to a more spiritual place in your life.

If you truly know in your heart you have no proficient degree of boxing or empty hand striking skills do *not* display your lack of skills on a prison punching bag. You will expose your weakness to the wolves and the ones who do have real training. However, if you do have extensive training and proficiency in empty-hand striking arts you may find occasion to incorporate an occasional bag workout into your cardio routine. But do not do it if the bag is in a gang hang out area or too many people are grouped around. Also, do not make a show of it or swagger afterwards. If asked do you know martial arts, or use to box, humbly say no. If pressed just say you do it for cardio only, but it would be wise not to jump out there and flex on the bag too soon. Wait until you've settled in to your environment and have a feel for the people around you. Sometimes power perceived can be power achieved. But never talk about, disclose, confide, or brag about your martial, or military, training. And never flex too much if you decide to work the heavy bag, as in show casing too much of your skills. Keep it simple, so that you get a good work out but don't reveal much of your skills. It's okay to show a little '*power*' to deter some of the wolves, but never reveal too much of your '*skill*'.

If you know in your heart that you're not extremely proficient do **not** ever expose your weakness by beating on a prison heavy bag. You wont deter anyone, but rather encourage some predators to target you. And rest assured that in prison few people are fighting with their empty hands. So if the wolves come they're coming deep, armed with shanks to let the air out of you with the element of surprise. If they decide they want to humble you, or hurt you, they wont be scared of one man regardless of his fighting prowess. They know that an armed sneak attack by multiple attackers can bring down the biggest and the baddest. Don't get cocky and comfortable and believe that you can't get butchered, or swarmed by enough strong men to be held down. And don't think your food can't be spiked by someone in the kitchen. The proper amount of power perceived combined with a humble attitude is the right combination. '*Walk in humble confidence*'.

In deterrence your greatest allies are to stay fighting fit, hide your smiles and cries, show **no** emotion (be stoic), be humble, be respectful, and create a quiet persona. I reiterate that the quiet reclusive type is treated with more caution than the loud, cocky, macho-tough individual. There is something intimidating about an individual in prison who is very quiet, calm, humble, and reveals no emotion in their face or eyes. It's not seen as 'normal' in a world of insanity. In fact it's viewed as 'crazy'. And the icing on the cake is to be seen only exercising daily, reading, writing, and doing you job. If you have to look at anyone speaking to you, or staring at you hard, try to look *'through'* them and nod a small respectful nod as a confident gesture of respect combined with strength. Convicts **and** guards always talk about the *'quiet ones'* as being the ones not to mess with. So being the *'quiet one'* is a strong deterrence, when combined with humble strength and a respectful, emotionless, attitude within the prison system. It is best that you recreate yourself with discipline and become this way for it's all a matter of survival.

Escape/Threat Neutralization is the final element to self-defense and sometime no matter how well you master the first five elements there may be a real fool, or group of fools, who just don't care if tomorrow never comes. And in prison you will find no shortage of these types. If you are heart checked, or attacked by wolves physically, you can not escape in prison. There's nowhere to run, but *sometime* you can choose the battlefield where you will make your stand. A small confined space is an advantage when facing multiple attackers. So retreating to your cell, or waiting in your cell, for an anticipated attack is not a bad idea. They may have to maneuver through a small channel of space, so flanking you will not be an available option and they will have to fight over each other to get to you. If you have been tipped off, or sense the attack coming, you can also prepare by sprinkling the floor entrance of your cell with baby powder or a slippery liquid to rob your attackers of their footing. If they can't stand they can't fight. Body armor to protect some of the major organs can be made by placing thick magazines or the covers taken from hardback books around your torso and secure it with ace bandages, or any long cloth, and place your t-shirt (or long john shirt) over it tucked into your pants. You want to cover the kidneys, liver, spleen, rib cage, and up to the solar plexus if you are able to acquire the material. Most of the time your attackers will be armed with shanks, ice picks, and knives. Some may attack with chemicals to burn the eyes and blind you. Or they may create a *'stinger'* to boil a cup of water and add magic-shave chemical hair remover, sugar, or grease to burn the meat off of one's body. A jacket, towel, or pillow can be held ready to act as a deflector or shield. A towel may be rolled up, wrapped around your neck, and tuck the ends down the front of your shirt, so that when you draw up your shoulders and take a fighting stance your carotid arteries, jugular vein, and carotid veins will be protected. Sunglasses will offer you some eye protection from chemicals, salt and pepper, or sand tossed into the eyes. A knit wool cap over your head and ears with a towel or shirt wrapped around the lower half of your face will complete your protective gear in case of an attack of boiled chemicals or oil (etc.). If you have gloves they'll offer your hands some protection but unless you have a shank of your own, your hands will be limited as defensive weapons during a counter attack. So gloves may limit you from utilizing finger strikes to their eyes, seizing strikes to their trachea, and neck-lock throws during a counter-attack.

I must point out that most of the time when you are forced to defend yourself in prison your adversaries will utilize the element of surprise and you will have to defend and counter attack in an instant. You will not have time to get prepared or put on much protective gear. So it is vital that one stay alert and pay attention to details. Expect the unexpected and you will never be surprised. Proper preparation entails your physical fitness training and conditioning, as well as your mental battle proofing. Make no mistake, prison is a warzone and you must be prepared to protect yourself at all times by any and all means available to you. Both psychologically and physically.

Unless you're highly trained in Israeli Krav Maga, Gutterfighting, Kapap or Aiki-jujitsu you're probably not equipped to deal with multiple attackers, whom are likely armed, in a real world combat situation. If you're a boxer or karateka than you may be able to hold your own (one on one) given that you see the attack coming, that the delicate metacarpal bones and knuckles of your hands are properly hardened and conditioned through constant Hojo Undo training, and your strikes are always perfect. But if they get in close and grapple with you, take you down, or you miss and break your hand on the hard bone of the skull, you're no longer combat effective.

Anyone whose watched the very first bare knuckle UFC brawls of the early 90's knows even 5th dan Kempo karate masters and professional boxers break their hands and get taken down to their back by wrestlers. (*And this is against single unarmed opponent!*) In prison you will up against experienced multiple attackers. If only one individual comes at you by their self it's only a *'heart check'*, unless of course they are armed.

Always assume that every attacker in prison is armed because most stabbing victims never see the weapon. Many do not even know they're being stabbed at the time, but believe they're only being beaten with punches. Never the less, in prison get into the habit of watching everyone's hands. If *'any'* attack comes it will come from the hands, be it a fist or a weapon. Usually you can 'feel' an attack before it comes. Learn to push out with your feelings and sense the intentions and aggression in others. Anyone who comes near you watch their hands and their body language. Don't be distracted by their face or voice because they will use that as a diversionary tactic. Watch the hands and body for any subtle signs of an attack. Hidden hand under a towel, magazine, or behind the leg (etc.) are a **few** examples.

In a fight you want to be careful not to break the small delicate bones in the hand. One will need to condition the hands with pull-ups, push-ups, fist push-ups, finger tip push-ups, and tiger claw push-ups to harden and strengthen the hands beyond normal. But do not fool yourself, the human skull is rounded and harder than brick. Being rounded means that the force of the impact will **not** be evenly distributed across the knuckles of your 'punch'. Your conditioned hands and fingers can break ribs, rupture internal organs, break jaws, gouge eyes, crush or tear out the tracheal wind pipe, and rip through soft tissue of the face and neck. But they'll still break against the hard bones of a fast moving human head. I've learned from experience.

A fight is close, frantic, and dirty. Forget all the junk you see in the movies or the school yard scraps you may have won or lost. In close quarter hand-to-hand combat the rule of thumb is to use speed, surprise, and violence of action to neutralize any attacker with a minimal amount of strength and effort. For instance, a thumb into the eye is more effective than a punch to the face in stopping or deterring an aggressor. An elbow strike to the chin, eye, or nose generates more power and force of impact than a closed fist. A heel-palm tiger claw strike generates more force than a knuckle punch to the chin, nose, or tempro mandibular joint without the risk of breaking the delicate metacarpal bones in the hand. The 'heel' of the palm is composed of dense carpal bones, made denser by elevated push-ups and body dips, that make it much more suitable to striking facial targets of an attacker during a fight.

In military close quarter/ hand to hand combat we believe in preserving the hands. (Never throw fists to the face!) In a real combat situation you will use fist strikes to the body/torso targets; the floating ribs, kidneys, liver and solar-plexus.

You will utilize the heel-palm tiger claw strikes, impacting with the heel of the hand, to the facial targets; chin, nose bridge, tmj, steno mastoid, the ear, temple, and the eye socket.

You will use thumb and/ or fingers to viciously gouge the eye ball, or seize and violently squeeze the trachea wind-pipe. It is expedient to keep a small bit of nail on your thumb to facilitate tearing out or rupturing an attacker's eye ball. (Remember you're fighting for you're life.) It isn't necessary to kill an armed attacker and catch a manslaughter charge. Just maiming, crippling, or knocking your attacker out is enough to neutralize and move on to the next attacker. If you're fortunate, the others may even back down, if you hurt the first one bad enough and quickly enough.

To form a heel-palm tiger claw get down into push-up position and while your palms are flat on the floor curl your fingers and thumbs until the tips are digging into the concrete and all of the weight is supported on the 'heel' of the hand. This is the way you'll do tiger claw push-ups in order to condition and train the hands to utilize the 'heel-palm' strikes. By curling the finger tips and thumbs into a tiger-claw position the 'heel' of the palm protrudes into the correct position to deliver a strike to the facial targets: chin, bridge of the nose, jaw, tempro mandibular joint, ear, and/or steno-mastoid. It's important to keep the thumb in tight to the hand while doing the tiger claw push ups and when striking with this palm formation so as not leave the thumb out where it's susceptible to injury.

To form a proper fist you want to curl your finger inward, until your hand is closed, and secure it by folding the thumb inward across the index and middle finger tightly. To condition the fists for punching into the softer targets of the torso get down into the push-up position while resting all of the weight of your upper body upon the index and middle knuckles of your fists. Next you will rotate the fists so that the thumb side is at your twelve o'clock and the second, third, and fourth knuckles are in contact with the ground, supporting all of your weight. You will perform push-ups in this position as well to condition these knuckles and metacarpal bones. The knuckles are your weapons for striking the softer targets of the solar-plexus below the sternum to stop breathing or create a knock-out, to break the short floating ribs, bruise the kidneys, or rupture the liver and cause a knock-out or disabling effect upon your attacker.

To execute a 'proper' punch your feet should be little more than shoulder width with one foot in front of the opposite foot, but off set at 'almost' a 45degree angle between the toes of the back and front foot. To give you an illustration just stand in front of the wall and place your hands against the wall and try to physically push down the wall. To generate enough force you will have to change your stance so that one leg is behind the other. This is the driving leg that pushes up from the ground. Your forward leg should be so that the foot is just in front of the shoulder. As you throw your strike you will slightly step forward with the ball of your lead foot, landing on the ball, as you drive from the rear foot and deliver the strike to your vulnerable target. The power comes up from the toes of the rear foot, through the leg to the knee, rotate the hip into the strike, torque the abdomen, drive from the latimus dorsis (wings) of the back muscle, in from the elbow, down the flexed forearm, driving the first two knuckles of your tightened fist into the vulnerable torso targets. Before impact, you will rotate your fist into the targets to generate maximum force of impact by creating a 'snap' at the end of your body punch. The left fist will rotate clockwise, while the right fist will rotate counter clockwise. This is called a reverse punch or twisting punch. It's very good for torso targets like the ribs. To throw the straight-punch just keep the thumb side up and the little finger side down as you drive in with the punch. You must be able to hunt your targets with calm, vicious, deliberation. **The best defense is a strong offense.** The same mechanics pretty much apply to throwing any hand (or elbow) strike when it comes to generating power from the rear foot and up through the body. I will note that the straight punch, once practiced, generates more power because you have the weight of your entire body behind it, as opposed to the reverse (twisting) punch which only has the strength of the shoulder behind it. However, the twisting punch allows for the index and middle knuckles to land between the ribs when striking to the floating (short) ribs.

One's greatest weapon in a combat situation is **surprise**. So whatever skills you have must be shrouded in total secrecy and you must allow your enemies to feel over confident.

Your most effective tools in close quarter hand-to-hand combat will be vicious, swift, attacks directed at your attacker's trachea (wind pipe), eyes, and ears. The biggest muscleman will be helpless if you seize the trachea swiftly and aggressively squeeze it like you would crumple a soda pop can. Anyone who has seen a big guy accidently catch a pinky finger in the eye during a basketball game can attest to the effectiveness of an eye gouge. You need not be big or strong to thumb gouge, finger jab, or finger slash the eye ball of an attacker. Finger tip push-ups sill strengthen the phalanges and tiger claw push-ups will harden the finger tips.

Open the hand until the index finger and thumb form a 90% right angle in the web of your hand. The base knuckle of the index finger is the point of impact used to deliver a strike to the trachea of an attacker and induce choking. To deliver it properly the hand must rise upward and into the throat, just like you are trying to swiftly and violently grab your aggressor around the front of the neck with one hand. In fact, this open ridge-hand strike to the throat can be immediately followed with curling the thumb and first three fingers into and behind the trachea aggressively. Dig in and around until the thumb and finger tips touch to drop most any attacker with this single counter attack.

To neutralize or discombobulate an aggressor swiftly with minimal force one can attack both ears by smoothly, without warning, bringing both palms up and slapping the ears simultaneously, before seizing the trachea or gouging an eye in a counter-attack. The palms of the hands must be stretched tightly to create sufficient force to rupture the eardrums of an aggressor in close quarter combat. This is commonly referred to as 'boxing the ears'. Originally in 'fisticuffs', open hand palm strikes (cuffs) were used to attack the ear drums, fingers jabs to the eyes, and fists were reserved for the torso targets, such as solar plexus, liver, ribs, and the kidneys. This was the original self defense art which later was demilitarized, like most martial arts, by modifying the facial strikes into closed hand punches to make the fight less lethal, more bloody, and last longer for the ring for sporting purposes. Other martial arts modified the more lethal and maiming strikes into closed fist strikes for more humane civilian self defense where increased laws would punish a man for seriously maiming or killing an attacker in a street fight or brawl. However, this modification placed the street defender's, or ring fighter's, hands in greater jeopardy of mechanical injury during combat.

If one should end up somehow on the ground surrounded by attackers, most likely they will want to remain standing and kick you while you're down or bend over to punch you. One's best defense is to violently and continuously kick your heels into the shins of one's standing attackers to hyper extend or break their knee. In addition, another good technique is to use one foot to hook their ankle while violently shoving the heel of the opposite foot into their shin. Alternately one may also grab one of their ankles with on hand and pull, while driving the hard bone of the forearm of your opposite limb hard into their shin bone. All of these variable techniques will bring a standing attacker down from a supine or a kneeling position.

If grabbed from behind unexpectedly by an attacker you must respond immediately and deliberately. A hold around you neck from behind requires that you immediately tuck your chin and turn into the elbow of your attacker's arm,, while simultaneously side stepping and delivering a strike down and back into their genitals with the knife edge of your hand. As soon as you feel impact upon their genitals turn the hand into the area and grab violently. The shock should be enough to cause them to release you where you will turn into your aggressor and viciously counter-attack their trachea and/or eye.

A simple grab from behind and around your arms requires immediate reflexes where one must drop their weight into a squat position, feet wide, hips dropped, as you immediately lean over and look down between your feet for the nearest ankle of your attacker. You will seize that ankle with one or both hands, by any means necessary, and pull upward while sitting downward with your hips. This makes your body the fulcrum and your attacker's leg the lever, as you lock out their knee and cause their fall. You can practice this by holding your arms against the front of your body, dropping your hips, and grabbing a chair or bunk leg behind you repeatedly.

Another common grab from behind is where your attacker has you around the torso, perhaps off your feet, and one or both of your hands are free. The instant you're grabbed you will use the second knuckle of your middle finger, or index finger, to rapidly wood pecker strike the back of your attacker's hand until they let go. The back of the hand is full of nerves which make this very painful, but as soon as they release their hold you will turn into them and viciously counter-attack.

The only kicks you want to use are to the middle of the shin of an aggressor's lead leg, followed by an immediate counter-attack to the other more vital targets. You don't want to kick any higher and risk your foot being grabbed, or your attacker charging in while one foot is off the ground unbalancing you. Sometimes one may find an opportunity to fake an open hand finger jab strike at one's attacker's eyes and as they are distracted launch a front snap kick up into their testes with one's toe. But this usually is only meant to get them to either drop their hands so you may strike a more effective neutralization target, or group of targets, or disrupt their attention long enough to execute a take down or a choke. But this usually requires some level of practice and training experience. Ultimately you want to keep it simple and dirty in a real close quarter/hand-to-hand combat situation. **Fancy and pretty techniques don't win battles. Simple and vicious does. (Speed, surprise, and violence of action.)**

So far we've covered a select few counter 'offensive' techniques one may apply with great effect and minimal injury to one's hands. However, for the true fighter is not the one who knows how to strike but the one who knows how 'not' to be struck. Offensive techniques are not the cure-all of physical self defense. But for one whom is untrained they can be utilized with great effect, for it is said that if all else fails the best defense is a vicious offense.

Unless you already have training in trapping and redirection techniques it is foolish to presume one can learn and acquire the necessary proficiency to execute such techniques in a real combat situation against multiple attackers simply by reading a manual. That level of skill and confidence only comes by training and experience, particularly against multiple (armed) attackers who do not attack individually. For that type of training one needs to join a self-defense club and train extensively in either WWII Gutterfighting , Israeli Commando Krav Maga, Kapap, American

Combat Hapkido, and Takagi Shin Ryu Aiki-Jujutsu.

Some schools of Silat, such as Brunein Silat Suffian Bela Diri, focus upon multiple armed attacker defenses. But in my opinion Takagi Shin Ryu Aiki-Jujutsu and WWII Gutterfighting systems are the most practical arts. These systems emphasize re-direction and trapping techniques which are more combat efficient than 'blocking' techniques. Trying to 'block' a large, powerful, berserker with a butcher knife is not prudent and seldom effective in a real attack. It's more efficient and effective to trap or re-direct an attack, following with a swift aggressive neutralization technique. But given the limited context of this book and the assumption that one may already be incarcerated, here are a few simple tips to keep in mind when defending against one or more armed (or unarmed) attackers.

Self-defense/hand to hand combat is all about either creating space or closing the distance with an attacker. In confined spaces one may be limited in the ability to create much space between oneself and one's attackers. But one may always create space between oneself and 'the attack' it's self. For example, one may turn 'with' an attack and absorb it or re-direct it.

One principle is to step to either the outside or the inside of an attack and *flow* either *around* or *upon it.* Become like water. Nothing is softer or weaker than water, but for overcoming the hard and strong there is nothing like it! Don't think of 'stopping' an attack or a strike. Think in terms of 'flowing' around or upon it.

In a grappling situation become like water: the harder it is grasped the more elusive it becomes. Become like a spinning ball that turns with the force of a push or a punch, so as to absorb, dissipate, and re-direct the force of an attack. When pushed, turn. When pulled, enter in and flow around or upon your attacker. Again, become like water.

In a knife attack the weapon will either be swung wide, thrust downward in an ice pick motion, or thrust directly inward to your torso. To keep it simple, just attack the knife **and** simultaneously attack the aggressor with a vicious, swift, neutralization technique. As the attack comes in, strike the base of the attacker's thumb, wrist, or knock the weapon from their grip, as you simultaneously enter in with your free hand and either gouge an eye with a hard thumb nail or swiftly seize and squeeze their trachea (wind pipe) with vicious talons until they drop. Against multiple attackers you will want to use this first attacker's body as a buffer between yourself and others for a quick moment. As you neutralize one you may push their body into other attacker's to stop or hinder their attacks. You must understand that in combat you must no longer see them as predators and yourself as prey (or victim). They don't know it but now 'they' are the victims. When attacked by wolves one must become a wolverine. The predators will become the prey. Before their eyes you will change form, from a humble lamb to a snarling lion whom glories in battle. With a flip of a mental switch you will change from a humble monk of peace to a vicious and fierce human weapon against any who wish to prey upon you.

The moment you are attacked, or perceive an attack, you will initiate an immediate attack of your own using **speed, surprise, and violence of action.** If your aggressor makes to grab you, go for their trachea and lock down on it or go for their eyeball. When seizing the trachea it is expedient sometimes to use one hand to grab the back of their neck while the other hand seizes the trachea windpipe with prejudice. The key here is reckless abandonment when executing this attack. Commit to it and move in for the take down. If your aggressor swings wide, or open (as many do) you must close the distance quickly by lunging inside their swing so that now their weapon (punch or shank) is behind you. Lunge 'inside' and flow 'over' the attack as you seize the trachea, gouge an eye, or heel palm strike the chin. If you do heel palm strike the chin, or gouge the eye, rapidly transition to attack the trachea while their stunned. Make each attack flow in transition with quick exhales of breath. If you shout with each attack you will magnify your strength by as much as 27% and also stun your attacker psychologically for a split second.

It's imperative that you think in terms of stepping to the outside or inside. '*Stepping off-line* ', as we call it. A *wide swing* allows you to *step 'inside' and flow over* the attack. A *direct, straight, attack* like a shove, thrust, jab, or grab allows you to *step 'outside' and flow around the attack* as it begins to be thrust toward you. If grabbed or shoved one must *turn with the attack* so that you allow their force to dissipate beyond you *while placing yourself 'outside' the attack* for a split moment.

In a close quarter hand-to-hand combat situation the moment you sense an attack it's best that you make a pre-emptive strike and attack first, especially when facing multiple attackers and your life is danger. However, once you are in the fight, or see an attack about to happen, one must take a *defensive fighting stance*. (Protect yourself at all times.)

A good defensive stance must allow you stability with the potential for motion. Some prefer a wrestling stance, some a boxing stance, while some a karate stance. Personally, I prefer a modified kendo/ aikido 'Sankakutai' stance, which resembles a loose triangle stance. But a simple, practical, stance is best for anyone not thoroughly trained in combat arts and experienced in defending against multiple armed attackers. Begin by standing comfortably and relaxed. Take a short step behind with your right and place it down with most of the pressure on the front of the foot, the toes of the back foot pointing relatively to your two o'clock. Turn your front foot with your toes pointing between twelve and one o'clock as you slide slightly forward until you feel comfortably stable. Allow most of your weight to sit on the back foot with pressure on the ball of the front foot. Slightly bend the knees and lower you center of gravity into your hips. Raise the hands up and in front of you with elbows down and in close to the body. Hands should form a relaxed tiger claw position, as described earlier, with the left slightly forward of the right and both hands orientated toward your attacker (who has now become your target). Keep the chin drawn in and tucked with your jaw clenched. It's good to keep a tiny square of cloth handy, about the size of a piece of Dentine chewing gum, to put in your mouth and bite down on if you anticipate an altercation. The shoulders should be slightly raised and your gaze should be either on your attacker's chest, near the center, or at the base of your attacker's throat, once the attack or fight is in play.

When you lunge to enter in, or deliver a strike to a specific vital area, or close the distance and attack, **your back foot is the driving force.** Never extend your shoulders beyond your front knee or you will over extend yourself and lose balance. Remain centered.

When throwing a heel palm strike, you want to 'snap' the strike by retracting it at the moment of impact to create a concussion effect. Much like the snap of a whip. Don't lean into a strike. 'Step' into a strike, much like one steps into a baseball swing. When throwing an eye gouge keep the hand somewhat relaxed and flex upon impact. Once impact is made, commit to it and gouge with the nail. Or you can attack the nostrils of the nose.

To conclude our crash course in self-defense, hand-to-hand/ close quarter combat, keep in mind that when all else fails and one must resort to aggressive negotiation your best tools are **swiftness, surprise, and violence of action.** Your greatest ally is **the undying will to prevail.** Maintain the undying will to prevail!

Become a fox to avoid traps.

Become a lion to chase away wolves.

In one's physical training let us add that cardio and endurance are extremely important in being 'fighting fit'. Daily incorporate side-straddle hops (jumping jacks), squat thrusts, and jogging into your routine. **Proper preparation prevents poor performance.** In a close quarter combat situation against multiple attacker's you don't want to run out of gas before they do. It will cost your life. You are in a warzone now, so you must become disciplined and always prepared.

Wide arm pull-ups, push-ups, body dips, lunges, deep knee bends, sit-ups, crunches, and stretching exercises all strengthen & condition the muscles used in close combat. Another vital exercise to remember is one's combat breathing exercises. Particularly when confronted by an aggressive personality or potentially violent situation.

Breath is mind.

Mind is breath.

Return to the breath.

As a final piece of advice, if one does find themselves in a self defense combat situation and end up going to the 'hole' (solitary confinement) for fighting, but for your own safety can not tell the administration the details of the altercation and be labeled a 'snitch' by other prisoners. Simply tell them you were protecting yourself and you can't say anymore. You will be placed under investigation and all of your outgoing mail and phone calls will be monitored by internal affairs. Write any details you need the administration to know about in a letter to a family member or friend on the outside and mail it out. If you're allowed a phone call you can discuss the details over the phone with family or friend and the internal affairs people listening will get the details of the incident indirectly while you will not be directly talking to the police. This way you're protected from being labeled a snitch and possibly killed by the gangs and predators in the penal system. If the administration try to interview you directly you tell them you're not a snitch and got nothing to say except that you were protecting your life, end of story. Keep in mind that some of the administration are in business with the gangs and you can't trust anyone in the system. They will be reading and possibly copying your outgoing mail, so they can get your side of the story indirectly as they intercept your mail and phone calls. **Always think outside of the box and walk softly (but keep your hands heavy).** *Wisdom is the best self-defense of all.*

Chapter 6.

LOOKING FOR A FEW MEN

For this subject I've chosen a popular recruitment slogan to illustrate the method of seduction and propaganda one will encounter in prison with the various gangs, organizations, and 'families'. Some use intimidation, fear, and threat to gain new recruits. Many use propaganda, manipulation, and seduction to gain recruits. They will watch and observe you for awhile and psychology profile you to discern what your needs are. If you seem shaky they'll offer protection. If you appear lonely they'll offer camaraderie and family like unity. If you seem insecure they will offer support and build your confidence. If you're indigent they'll show you generosity for a season, and if you're greedy they'll show you a seemingly better way to gain your desires. If you're angry they will offer you vengeance and give you an enemy to direct that anger at. If you enjoy violence they'll offer you a life of it. If you're proud they'll stoke your ego. If you're looking for meaning and not sure who you are they will tell you that you are a warrior, a soldier, a special being, a super being.

So many individuals get lured in so seductively and never see the reality of the situation until it's too late. Like being led down a gold brick road that leads to more misery, pain, and misfortune, but one can't see it until it's too late. They'll tell you that they don't take just 'anyone' into their organization, but they like the way you carry yourself. They still need time to watch you and check you out though. They only accept strong, intelligent, real individuals. If you're not the best of the best you can't be in their elite circle. They're hated by many but respected by all. They may want to teach you secret knowledge very few possess. They may know who and what you really are (they claim) and want to tell you 'when you're ready'. They may tell you that they're revolutionaries fighting political, economic, and racial oppression. Some will tell you that they go back to ancient times and will feed you a story of their origin and how they've become who they are today in the present times. Most of them have wonderful stories that are a creative mix of factual history and creative propaganda. Some have absurd stories that appeal only to the delusional mind. They all use images, because images influence the mind.

The truth is that despite all the hype, rhetoric, propaganda, they are all thugs and terrorist. And none of them want to recruit you for your best attributes and abilities. They want you for your worst. In a criminal organization, gang, 'family', or cult there is no peace, joy, prosperity, or love. Only strife, disfunction, hate, fear, betrayal, treachery, and destruction until the end. A good illustration would be a candy coated fece; sweet attraction on the outside and bitter disgust on the inside.

At first they will appear to be trying to make you a better person physically, mentally, and maybe even spiritually. They will give you gifts, but you will not see the hooks in it meant to reel you in. By accepting any gift they will feel that you're now obligated to them (even when they say that you wont be). They will teach you how to work out and get physically fit, to carry yourself with pride, to become more disciplined like a military soldier. They will teach you 'secret knowledge' and interesting skills of creativity. They slowly want you to become indoctrinated and assimilated until you're no longer an individual, but another part in their machine. It's a growing process of seduction. It's like a pyramid scheme. Despite the propaganda of unity, loyalty, and camaraderie, the purpose of the whole thing is to serve and feed a select few (or individual) at the tip of the pyramid empire. They do not really seek to help the people at all. That is a lie. It is all about the hierarchy getting rich and feeding their monstrous ego at the expense of others. And these leaders are living in a paranoid wilderness of mirrors, so 'anyone' with too much charisma or ambition within their organization (or whatever they call it) will be seen as a threat to the leadership at the tip of the pyramid. And the charismatic or ambitious personality will be betrayed and taken out to maintain their security.

Usually by the time the individual has a moment of parapettio it is too late. One is in too deep. If an epiphany is a momentary sensation of stupidity, than sooner or later that is what awaits every soul that sells itself to the bidding of an egomaniac.

If they succeed in recruiting you everything will change. You will be given orders and to refuse will have consequences. Whatever freedom the prison administration did not take from you will now be lost. You will be ordered to force large packs of drugs, contraband, weapons, and even cell phones into your colon to hold in case of a surprise shake down and strip search by the guards. If you get caught with any of it, and the guards confiscate it, you are responsible for replacing or paying for whatever was lost while in your possession. (No excuses.) They will expect you to manipulate even your family for the benefit of the organization. They don't care about 'you'. You're expendable to the hierarchy.

You could be a couple years, or a couple of months, from completing your sentence and going home to your children who need you but they will order you to carry out a murder on one of their rivals, or enemies, and if you refuse they will do you or have a hit put on your family members. No negotiations. And you will now earn a life sentence and never know freedom again.

Perhaps they may encourage you to lay low in prison, if you're a good earner, because you can be of more further use to them on the street, but in the long run the same rules apply and the end is the same. There is no future but 'Life' sentence in prison, the I.C.U., and an early grave when you get involved with a criminal organization of any kind. They only want puppets and send-outs to serve their ego and greed.

A more appropriate recruitment slogan would be, 'We are looking for a few good send-outs and crash dummies.'

There's nothing positive they can't do for you that you can't do for yourself. Nothing positive they can teach you to make you stronger and smarter that you can't learn on your own. You can exercise and train yourself without them. You can read and study the same books that they do, on your own. Books like: The Art of War by Sun Tzu, Tao Te Ching by Lao Tzu, 48 Laws of Power-Art of Seduction-33 Strategies of War by Robert Green, Book of Five Rings by Miyamoto Musashi, Dictates of a Warrior by Marcus Areoleous, Law books, medical books, and religious books. (Just to name a few). You can train and educate yourself to be stronger, more intelligent, and definitely wiser than any of them all on your own.

Throughout history, until the present day, and in various cultures there have been warrior societies. These warriors are servants who devote themselves to a life of discipline, self-less service, and altruistic love for the good of their society, their families, and their people. A warrior protects the weak, the elderly, the widows, the children, the women, the oppressed. A warrior will sacrifice their desires, and needs even, so that others wont suffer without. A warrior fights against oppression, and ensures the survival and needs of the women, children, and elderly are met. A warrior sees that the needs, security, and safety of the people is met, even at the cost of himself.

A criminal organization (in contrast) destroys the people. They exploit the women, children, and elderly. They poison the people with drugs and terrorize with fear, even their own people. They live only for their selfish desires at the expense of others. They rob the people of their sons and daughters. They create widows and rob the mothers of the children who would care for them in old age. They provide the people with insecurity and danger in their own villages and neighborhoods. They create oppression upon their own people. Rather than make life easier they make life more difficult for the people. Rather than cultivate the minds of the young ones, they pollute them with drugs, alcohol, violence, greed, and evil. They do not walk in the tradition of a warrior, but pervert the significance of this title in order to lure the young and seduce them with a glorified and romanticized culture of thuggery and barbarianism. They do not improve their people or society but rather contribute to the degeneration of society, their peoples, and the family at home. This is not the traditional role of warriors.

Do not be seduced by the criminal organization, gang, crime 'family', or cult organization in prison.

Let me add in closing that once you are confirmed as a member of any of these organizations any new charges will be enhanced at sentencing by the court under the anti-terrorism act. And any chances of parole will be diminished, if not nullified. You will not ever be allowed to transfer to a minimum security facility where you can do easier time and enjoy more privileges. They will only make hard time harder for you in the long run.

The key to surviving prison is to make your time as easy as possible, not harder. You give respect to everyone. Let no one abuse you. Don't spit in the sink. Stand with your back to the door if you have any bodily gases that need release. Clean up after yourself. Clean up your cell and don't expect your cellee to do it all time for you. Be quiet when your cellee is resting his eyes or sleeping. Never cut in line: Wait your turn. Be courteous but don't be too nice. Don't ever smile at anyone. Don't snitch and mind your own business. Don't get in debt. Don't gamble. Don't talk to sissies or punks. Don't join a gang, or criminal organization. Treat others as you wish to be treated.

Chapter 7.

HUSTLERS, CONS, AND PSYCHIC VAMPIRES

Prison is a concentrated criminal community full of every type of criminal imaginable. Naturally there is no shortage of hustlers and cons waiting to run game and pop corn on you. Just remember, 'Don't Trust Anyone.'

In prison, just as in life, anything that sounds too good to be true always is. A major hustle you will encounter is the 'jail house lawyers'. A jailhouse lawyer almost always will have several people helping in the game who will act as promoters and tell you, directly or indirectly, how good 'So and So' is with the law. They will all swear 'so and so' got someone off of death row and a life sentence off of themselves. They will even tell you they are about to go home their self thanks to this cold prison litigator. They may tell you also this prison litigator is about to go home soon because they gave time back to the courts, so you need to get with them soon to look over your case. And often they will tell you this individual either doesn't charge, or wont charge you very much.

Once they introduce you to this individual the jail house lawyer may pretend to be uninterested in taking on anymore cases, or may pretend to be so close to going home they don't have time. They may look over your paper work and pretend to find a loop hole in your indictment, the jury instruction, or the sentence of judgment. First, they want to look over your paper work to see if your social security number is anywhere. **They want this so they can steal your identity.** Secondly, they want to find a discrepancy in your paperwork they can exploit to convince you that you can get out of prison and get your case overturned. At first they may tell you they need no payment but as time goes on they will maybe try to make you feel obligated to show some appreciation for their helping you. **This is how they slow bleed you.**

Another scam is to tell you they have a lawyer friend who is gonna take your pro. se. petition and go to court and take your case pro. bono. with out charge. They may put you on a phone with another con playing a street lawyer who needs your family to send some money to his or her firm in order for them to post an 'appeal bond' on a writ of habeas corpus appeal. They'll lead you to believe you will be released on 'appeal bond' and then be out with your family while they'll continue to fight your case (which is guaranteed to be overturned.) The address you think is a law firm is actually an empty lot, or empty home, where someone will be waiting to sign for the fed ex postal money when mail runs on the outside. This 'attorney' friend of the jail house lawyer may tell you over the phone, or in an official looking letter, that they need your family's phone number so they may keep your family abreast on your case or to explain to your family how this 'appeal bond' may work. They actually want this so that they can con your family out of money, convince your family to go take out a loan for the 'Appeal bond', or even extort your family by making them fear for your life or theirs. All jail house lawyers are hustlers and con artists. Some play the short game and others play the long game. But it's all 'game'.

Another common con is someone will first try to earn your confidence and then they will either try to convince you that you can file for income tax return owed you , or they will try to convince you they have a relative who works for the IRS and they will help you to file for income tax return owed you for the last year that you worked in the free world. They will offer to help you fill out the form (so they can steal you SSN) or they may try to convince you to let them mail it to their relative who works in the IRS who will take care of everything. This is a hustle and a con. They only want to steal your identity and use it for crime, or sell your identity to criminals. You can not file income tax from within prison (legally).

Most con artist will try to earn your friendship and/or your confidence. In the older days a con-man was referred to as a 'confidence' man. This refers to the con-artist's act of winning the confidence of their victim in order to successfully carry out the con. So be very wary of anyone who wants to befriend you or earn your confidence. In prison no one is your friend, and no one has any reason to want to earn your trust or confidence but a con artist.

A lot of individuals will tell you, for example, let me borrow a bag of cookies and I will repay you next week. They may pay you back and immediately ask for something greater with the promise of repaying you.

Since they just repaid a dollar worth of cookies, their word is good, so you give them maybe five to ten dollars worth of other items on credit not knowing you will never see it all back. They may repay you two or three dollars and tell you they'll have the rest in a couple days, but until then let them get a bag of instant coffee and some cookies. They're hustling you, and if you allow it to continue they will slow bleed you dry. You're their 'duck'.

Another popular con is to ask you to hold something for them for a few minutes and they'll pay you for your trouble. Shortly after having taken upon yourself to hold whatever item they paid you to hold either a gang of armed individuals will rob you , or the police may run down on you and take the contraband. Now you owe this individual who is a gang member for the item you lost. So in order to repay the gang you have to work it off. Now they got you in their pocket. What you don't know is that they set you up to get caught holding something for them, and have it confiscated by the police or robbed by another gang, just so that you would owe them and become their mule or whatever else they want you to do for them. It was a set up from the jump.

Some individuals will play the friendly role, or the compassionate role, and give you hygiene items you may need, stamps & stationary, commissary, etc. etc. Once you seem semi-comfortable with them (and maybe their associates) they'll create a pretext for argument or act like you've offended them. Then they will announce that you owe them for everything they've given you and better have their stuff by a certain time frame. If you claim to be able to get it all back they will tell you they want the 'same' stuff back that they gave you. This is just a pretext for prison rape, or enslavement. **Don't accept anyone's charity! And if it is charity you don't owe them 'anything'! (Remember, D.T.A..)**

Another common con game is to tell you that they can't have money sent to their books (inmate account) because the court is taking it for payments of fees. So they'll ask you to allow their money to be sent to your account and then you can order commissary or other items for them off of your account. If you agree to this they will either try to exceed the amount that was sent to your account, and cause an altercation, or they will claim a specific amount was sent to your account (but it was not) and better order the items the want that amount to the sum of money they insist their family sent to you or there's gonna be a killing. They will insist you are trying to steal from them. So it is wise to not do 'anyone' any favors in prison.

There is a con game where your cell mate may send someone to the cell when you are there and that person will tell you that your 'cellee' said the could get something. If you assume it to be true and let them take it your cellee will later show up and accuse 'you' of stealing and insist that you now owe them. Usually this cellee is a gang member and it was a set up meant to intimidate you into becoming in debt to them so they can put you to work as their mule, duck, or send-out. Sometimes it's a pretext for extortion, or rape. Never let 'anyone' get any of your cell mate's personal property. Simply tell them to come back later when your cellee is in and get it from them directly. You live in that cell and your cell mate did not tell you anything about it, so you will not put yourself in a position of responsibility by allowing someone to come get something of your cellee's when they're not present.

Some old convicts fighting their case will use other prisoner's cases as a guinea pig. Either they'll offer to help you file something, like a habeas corpus relief petition, in court or tell you how to file it pro.se. Pro. se. means to do it by yourself. But they will want to see that you raise a particular issue, perhaps a specific way, that is similar to an issue they wish to raise in their own case. Since they may have only one proverbial bullet in their gun to shoot at the federal court they want to save it until they feel ready to file their own writ of habeas corpus. If you get some play on the issue they have suggested to you to raise then they plan to piggy back off of that same issue as well. If you don't, then they will just try a different formula and another person to raise it in their appeals. This is how they vicariously experiment with the courts through other people's cases until they find a key that will unlock the door, and 'then' they will feel ready to file their own writ of habeas corpus and take it all the way through state and federal levels for relief.

Now we should address the individuals that I've referred to as 'psychic vampires', whom seem to infest the prison system. Some are not only prisoners, but prison administration as well.

A 'psychic vampire' is an individual who gets a thrill to, or feels a need to, feed off of the emotions, mental stress, and/or pain of others. They try to keep you stressed or mentally and emotionally discombobulated. They seem to enjoy pushing people's buttons in order to keep them stressed, angry, depressed, discouraged, and even afraid. They feed off of others emotions and pain. They take pleasure in trying to drive others crazy or keep others emotionally upset.

If you feel stressed and left drained every time an individual comes around than this person is a psychic vampire.

If an individual always tries to get close to you and engage you in conversation, then studies you to find what your buttons are and pushes them, *this individual is a psychic vampire.*

If an individual seems to only come around every time you are at your low points; sad, upset, angry, or got some bad news. If they seem to be overly interested in your bad news and personal problems, but seem to be uninterested in your good news and blessings. If they seem to thrive on your stress, misery, and anger like an energy parasite or spiritual leech. Than be not mistaken for this individual 'is' a psychic vampire.

You must be able to recognize the characteristics and symptoms of a psychic vampire because such individuals are a very real threat to your mental, spiritual, and physical health. Nothing can make your time harder than a psychic vampire. If you are forced to cell with such an individual put on your mask and avoid conversation with them. And if you get the chance to move to another cell you may want to do so as soon as possible. If you are forced to stay with them do your best to give them nothing to feed upon. Show no emotion and hide you smiles and cries. Pretend nothing they say or do upsets you and show no emotion. Share nothing of yourself, your life, or your likes and dislikes with them. Give them 'nothing' to feed upon, and let them whither up and withdraw into their own misery. Become emotionally sterile and return the breath.

Doing time is hard enough mentally, emotionally, and physically without letting a psychic vampire drain you and stress you even more. Stress is the number one killer in the country. Stress causes strokes, cancer, heart disease, bowel illness, post traumatic stress disorder, peptic ulcers, and a host of other physical and mental illnesses that can lead to death. Psychic vampires are dangerous to your survival so avoid them at all cost and shun them. Your life is at stake here, so don't play their game and don't give them a foot hold. They are perhaps the most dangerous of all predators in a more subversive way, much akin to a parasite. They will begin by befriending you so they can learn all your pet peeves, dislikes, quirks, and weaknesses. They want to know all of your buttons. They will flip the script on you and start doing and saying little things to push these buttons. They'll even tell others what your buttons are and encourage them to get their own little cuts and jabs in. It's similar to the way the picadors weaken a Spanish fighting bull first with little darts and cuts, as they tease and provoke him, until he is finally weak and out of his mind. Then the matador can go in for the kill.

Don't trust anyone in the concrete jungle. In prison, even the sheep have fangs…Your 'only' friend is God. (Whether you know Him or not.)

CONCLUSION

Hopefully by now after reading thus far you have learned enough tools and knowledge to help you survive *the demon farm* that they call 'prison' and facilitate your time building. I can only describe it as part warzone and part human time capsule...But you 'can' make it your monastery, or a place of physical training and higher learning. When you change the way you look at things the things you look at change. It may take time, but know in your heart that you can survive anything. You will grow stronger with every great opposition. Like a diamond, you too must endure heat and pressure to change form a lump of coal into a strong, hard, and beautiful jewel that is able to reflect light. But it takes time, for no good thing comes quickly or easily. A warrior and a scholar both are forged by discipline and adversity over time. The most important thing is to cultivate and maintain a positive attitude and an undying will to prevail.

The techniques and knowledge in this book was acquired by the author during both his military career and fourteen years of incarceration for an attempted homicide. The author was still incarcerated at the time of writing this book but has transposed it to type after his supervised release back into the free world. At the time of writing this while still doing time, having survived well **over** a decade in general population, the knowledge & techniques in this manual are tried, field tested, and proven by the author. It is his hope that in writing this book that prisoners new to the system wont have to learn 'the hard way' and may avoid the pitfalls that await them in prisons, and even jails. Also it is hoped that this book may save lives and contribute to more peace within the penal system. As well as within the individual who finds their self doing the time.

It is said that one can lead a horse to water but can't make it drink, that being said the knowledge and techniques in this book only work if studied, practiced, and applied to one's daily life. Like anything it requires self-discipline.

The knowledge and tools in this autobiographical manual, of sorts, will get one very far, but the author would like to confess that there is a time that every individual can reach their 'breaking point.' When, that time should come the individual **will** need faith and hope in something greater than their self.

In his thirty five years the author has practiced and studied various religious and spiritual paths, including his traditional native American religion, shaman spirituality, the Native American Church, Protestant Christianity, Catholicism, Gnosticism, Sorcery, Tibetan Buddhism, Shambalic Path, Sunni Islam, Bushido, (and other things) before realizing that there is only one way, truth, and light. Today the author's best and only friend, during the writing of this book within his prison cell, is the Creator Lord Y'e'shua Christ Tsisas (Jesus). And the author through much scholarly research has found the King James translation to be the most accurate

English translation and the Reina Valera to be the most accurate Spanish translation of the Hebrew massaretic text, and the textus receptus.

Rather than 'discourage' you from seeking for yourself the author would 'encourage' you to study, read, and seek for yourself what is the perfect truth. Truth may be found in **all** things because every good lie must contain a portion of truth for it to be believable. But does one want a portion of truth, or the whole Truth and nothing but the truth?

Many want to claim a religion that is more ethnocentric to our ethnic background. Or a religion that is more tolerant and palatable to our desires and proclivities. So with this rigid attitude we harden our hearts and close our minds to anything outside of our preconceived notions or prejudices. We are so worldly minded and ethnocentric as people that we cripple ourselves, we cripple our hearts and minds. We want something that gives us an identity, reaffirms our identity, makes us feel good, or will serve us in our desires. We as people love rituals, aestheticism, secret knowledge, and the ascetic. We also love anything that promises us earthly desires fulfilled. We love to feel unique and special, or even superior to others. We sometimes want to assimilate others to '*our way*'.

Religion is man made for the most part and infested with wolves in sheep's clothing and hypocrites. (**All religions with out exception.**) But do not let those insurgents discourage or deceive you from your personal journey to find the Truth. It is 'your' journey and ultimately 'your' soul at stake, so let not others take the reins of your mind and heart. Personally myself, I do not follow a man made religion but have a personal 'faith' which I live by and follow in my daily life. That is where my personal journey has taken me and my sincere search for truth has brought me.

One thing is certain in this life dear friend. Whatever it is that you seek after, with all of your heart, you 'will' find. Be it good, or evil in life. Be it truth, half-truth, or self-deception. Be it peace, inner joy, and blessings. Be it something else all together. (Seek and you will find.)

The author encourages you to study books of all religions and seek with a sincere heart for the 'complete Truth'. But the author also would like to encourage you to write to: GARRETT FOUNDATION, P.O. Box 1453, Bessemer AL 35021. They will send prisoners FREE copies of the book THE IMAGE OF GOD upon request. This little book is extremely enlightening and thoroughly written. May it touch *your* life in a major and positive way, as it did this author's. Your journey is personal and it is your own.

Many people report seeing and experiencing negative entities in prison. Some experience a feeling of being immobilized, smothered, suffocated, choked, hit, and even unable to speak, by some unseen force in the night time. Some report seeing a shadowy human silhouette in the corner and feeling a very negative, even frightening, presence in the cell. Some hear a voice call to them in their ear and frighten them. Some have terrible night mares.

If you should ever be one who experiences anything like what we have just described, do 'not' tell a prison nurse or doctor. They are not equipped, or even aware of such things, to help you. You are 'not' crazy, so letting them deem you to be so will only make your time worse than it is.

Psychotropic medication (drugs) will compound what you are experiencing and will not liberate you from any negative spiritual entities, demons, or oppressive/depressive spiritual forces. It will not remove any negative spiritual haunting in your life.

The only thing that ever really works long term is to call upon the name of the Creator, Lord Jesus (In any language). Sage, tobacco, salt, ashes, symbols, incantations, prayer beads, crucifixes, pictures, chants, (etc.) will not work against these forces.

This may all sound crazy to some, but should you ever experience any of this you will know how to combat it. **And then you will learn the Truth.** So please just keep this in mind, whether you believe it or not, for perhaps someday you may need it.

One final book the author would like to recommend to the seeker, the curious, and scholar is, 'BY DIVINE DESIGN' written by Michael Pearl. A very good work of scholarship and intellectual reasoning for anyone seeking knowledge and is on a path for truth.

Well dear friend, you now possess an eclectic array of knowledge and potential tools that will give you an advantage 'very few' individuals have had prior to or upon entering incarceration.

These potential tools and knowledge can, and perhaps will, save one's life and imbue one with stress management techniques that will serve well both within and without, whether on is trying to survive the stresses and dangers of incarceration or the free world.

Some dictionaries define luck as 'when preparation meets opportunity', so good luck and D.T.A...Walk softly and maintain the undying will to prevail one day at a time. A journey of a thousand miles is made one step at a time. And the only easy day is yesterday.

Look for the positive even in the negative. And be grateful to the Creator for the food, water, air, sunlight, and health that you have been given. Be grateful for the little blessings and be content with what you have in your life.

Adversity and opposition are not your enemies, but rather your teachers. And character is destiny, so be the master of your own destiny.

They can lock up your body but they can't lock up your mind.

De Oppresso Liber.

ABOUT THE AUTHOR

Author N. Cognito is a pseudonym. The author of this book chooses to remain anonymous for personal reasons. Mr. N. Cognito was incarcerated in a C.C.A. prison for the conviction of first degree attempted homicide and survived the demon farm for more than a decade during the writing of this book. However during the transposition of the book to typed print Mr. N. Cognito is currently on supervised release.

Before his incarceration Mr. N. Cognito worked for the U.S. government, serving in an elite military unit, was a close combat / self defense instructor, U.S. Army Amateur boxer, renown visual tracker, and a member of the Native American Church.

Prior to his military career he was a semi-pro bull rider for the Texas Raw Courage Rodeo Circuit, a lifelong practitioner of the combat arts, bush craft, natural medicines, and shiatsu, while growing up with a deep interest in languages and a passionate love for nature and his native people and culture.

Today (at the time of his incarceration) Mr. N. Cognito is a born again soldier for the Kingdom of God and disciple of The Creator, Lord Christ Jesus, his best friend. His days are spent studying the Authorized King James Holy Bible, reading books by the author Michael Pearl and Dr. James P. Gills, writing his son, fighting an unconstitutional conviction, translating for non-English speaking prisoners and helping them fight for Constitutional/human rights within the penal system, exercising and awaiting the eminent return of the Lord, Our Creator, Christ Tsisas (Jesus).

The author is a living testament to the knowledge and techniques shared in this book. He hopes his experience and knowledge will save lives.

His son, **Emmanuel**, personal experiences, and Mike Pearl (who visited him in prison each week) were inspirations for the writing of this book. Written manuscript completed 9 October 2010 and transposition completed on 2 June 2013.

"Let us all be the change we wish to see in the world."